200 healthy chinese
recipes

hamlyn | all color cookbook

200 healthy chinese recipes

An Hachette UK company
www.hachette.co.uk

First published in Great Britain in 2013 by Hamlyn,
a division of Octopus Publishing Group Ltd
Endeavour House, 189 Shaftesbury Avenue, London WC2H 8JY
www.octopusbooks.co.uk

Distributed in the US by Hachette Book Group USA
237 Park Avenue, New York NY 10017 USA
www.octopusbooksusa.com

Distributed in Canada by Canadian Manda Group
165 Dufferin Street, Toronto, Ontario, Canada M6K 3H6
Copyright © Octopus Publishing Group Ltd 2013

Some of the recipes in this book have previously appeared
in other books published by Hamlyn.

ISBN: 978 0 60062 708 1

Printed and bound in China

1 2 3 4 5 6 7 8 9 10

Standard level kitchen cup and spoon measurements are
used in all recipes.

Ovens should be preheated to the specified temperature—
if using a convection oven, follow the manufacturer's
instructions for adjusting the time and the temperature.

Fresh herbs should be used unless otherwise stated.
Large eggs should be used unless otherwise stated.

The U.S. Food and Drug Administration advises that eggs
should not be consumed raw. This book contains some
dishes made with raw or lightly cooked eggs. It is prudent
for vulnerable people, such as pregnant and nursing moth-
ers, people with weakened immune systems, the elderly,
babies, and young children, to avoid uncooked or lightly
cooked dishes made with eggs. Once prepared, these
dishes should be kept refrigerated and used promptly.

This book includes dishes made with nuts and nut
derivatives. It is advisable for those with known allergic
reactions to nuts and nut derivatives and those who may
be potentially vulnerable to these allergies to avoid dishes
made with nuts and nut oils. It is also prudent to check the
labels of prepared ingredients for the possible inclusion of
nut derivatives.

contents

introduction

introduction

In China, food and its preparation have been developed so highly that it has reached the status of an art form. Both rich and poor Chinese people consider that delicious and nutritious food is a basic necessity of life.

The great ancient Chinese philosopher Confucius emphasized the artistic and social aspects of cooking and eating, and in China it is considered poor etiquette to invite friends to your home without providing something appropriate to eat. In fact, Chinese people simply don't gather together without there being food involved. The ancient Chinese philosophy of Taoism, on the other hand, encouraged research into the nourishment provided by food and cooking. Instead of concentrating on taste and appearance, Taoists were more interested in the health-giving and life-enhancing properties of food. Centuries on, the Chinese have discovered the health-promoting properties of all kinds of ingredients. They have taught the world that the nutritional value of vegetables is destroyed by overcooking (particularly boiling), and have discovered and demonstrated that ingredients with a great flavor also have medicinal value.

Home-cooked Chinese food is extremely healthy, because it uses only small quantities of polyunsaturated oils and excludes the use of dairy products. Many Chinese restaurants in the West prepare their menu using highly

saturated fats, but authentic Chinese food is arguably the healthiest on the planet. All the recipes in this book involve a minimal amount of oil, and most use low-calorie cooking spray.

The Chinese approach to cooking is one of the greatest there has ever been, and many factors have influenced its development from ancient times to the present day. Confucius once said, "Eating is the utmost important thing in life," and Chinese cuisine is considered a highly sophisticated art, requiring much time and consideration.

cooking styles: Beijing, Sichuan, Hunan, and Cantonese, but there are still many provincial variations and ethnic minority specialities.

Beijing
Beijing cuisine is also known as Mandarin cuisine. Many of the foods in this region are wheat-based (as opposed to rice-based), so Beijing cuisine consists of a variety of dumplings, baked and steamed breads, and various types of noodle. Mandarin-style meals usually include vegetable dishes, soups, tofu (soybean curd), and fish. The food is mild in taste, and vinegar and garlic are common ingredients. Dishes are frequently stewed or braised, while dumplings are filled with a meat or vegetable mixture and steamed.

A meal in Chinese culture is typically seen as consisting of two basic components: a main food, which is a source of carbohydrate or starch, typically rice (predominant in southern parts of China) or noodles (predominant in northern parts of China); and accompanying dishes of vegetables, seafood, fish, meat, and poultry.

Chinese regional cooking styles
China is a huge country geographically, and it is diverse in climate, ethnicity, and subcultures. Not surprisingly, there are many distinctive styles of cuisine. Historically, there were eight great culinary traditions (Anhui, Guandong, Fujian, Hunan, Jiangsu, Shandong, Sichuan, and Zhejian). Today, there are four main regional

Sichuan

Food from the Sichuan (or Szechuan, meaning "Four Rivers") basin is characteristic of the southwestern region of China. Featuring a liberal use of garlic, ginger, scallion, and chile, Sichuan food is distinguished by its hot, peppery flavors. It is the spiciest style of Chinese cooking and certainly tasty.

Hunan

The traditional cuisine of Hunan Province is richer than that of Sichuan and may be either spicy or sweet and sour. Chicken, pork, fish, and shellfish are all popular ingredients cooked in this manner.

Cantonese

From Canton or Guangdong Province in the southeastern region of China (which includes Hong Kong), Cantonese cuisine is the mildest and most widely consumed type of Chinese food in the world. Cantonese food tends to be more colorful and less spicy than the other regional styles of cooking and is usually stir-fried, which preserves both the texture and flavor of ingredients. Dim sum, or "tea lunch," usually consisting of tasty little dumplings and pastries stuffed with meats and vegetables, and it is served at many Cantonese restaurants during the lunch hour. Freshness is supreme to the Cantonese, and sauces are kept mild and subtle to avoid overpowering the fresh taste of the ingredients.

Healthy principles

The Chinese way of looking at health lies in one of the fundamental principles of its traditional philosophy, that food and medicine share the same roots. The firm belief that food has healing powers and therapeutic effects has led to the cultivation of many different edible plants and herbs in China, and as the benefits of disease prevention and health preservation that they offer have been recognized, so they have become standard ingredients in Chinese home-cooked dishes. At the same time, there has been a pursuit of refinement in Chinese cooking. The quantities of different ingredients and their combination are essential considerations. Whether making main dishes or soups, foods are combined according to their relative nutritional content to achieve the goal of an overall balance in nutritional intake. It is also recommended to eat only until the stomach is about 70–80 percent full, a practice that has been passed down through the generations as a secret to long life.

Equipment

The beauty of cooking Chinese food in your home is that you don't need much special equipment. The two main pieces of equipment are the wok and the bamboo steamer.

Wok

Key to Chinese cooking, the wok is the heart of the Chinese kitchen. There is almost no limit to the number of delicious dishes that can come out of this unassuming piece of equipment on the stove. It is one of the most useful and versatile pans available, because it can be used for stir-frying, blanching, and steaming foods as well as deep-frying. Its shape, with deep sides and a rounded bottom, allows for fuel-efficient, quick, even heating and cooking. This quick-cooking method also preserves the vitamins in the vegetables. Traditional-style woks need to be seasoned and tempered before using, but the recipes in this book feature a good-quality nonstick wok that doesn't need to be prepared before use and also requires the barest minimum of

oil for cooking, thus making your dishes even healthier. However, you can use a large, deep nonstick skillet in place of a wok.

Steamer

Steaming is essential to much of Chinese cooking. The best option is to buy one or more inexpensive bamboo steamers, which come in a wide range of sizes, with the 10 inch size being the most practical for the home cook. The food is placed in the steamer and that, in turn, is placed above boiling water in a wok or large saucepan. A tight-fitting bamboo lid prevents the steam from escaping.

To make the best use of your bamboo steamer, follow these simple instructions:

1 Fill the wok or saucepan about one-third with water. It is important that you use the right amount of water: too little and the water can boil off and scald the wok; too much, and it will boil up onto the food.

2 Bring the water to a boil over medium heat; wait until you see a rolling boil.

3 Carefully arrange your food inside the bamboo steamer—you can stack several bamboo steamer baskets on top of one another to cook different foods at the same time. Put food that cooks quickly in the top basket and food that takes a little longer in the bottom basket. Put the lid on the top basket.

4 Carefully place the steamer in your wok or pan. Let the water boil rapidly and circulate inside the steamer, evenly cooking the food. Cooking times will vary, depending on the food you are cooking.

5 Clean your bamboo steamers by washing them by hand with gentle dish-washing detergent and water. Don't soak them in the sink or put them in the dishwasher, because this can ruin the bamboo. Let the steamers air-dry completely before putting them away.

STEAMING TIPS

* Place a layer of cabbage or lettuce underneath the food in the steamer to prevent the food from sticking to the steamer, or line it with nonstick parchment paper. This is helpful when steaming sticky foods, such as dumplings or wontons.

* To avoid steam burns, always lift the lid of the steamer away from your body. Wrist burns can occur if steam or hot water are expelled as you lift the lid, so use caution. Use pot holders to set up and remove steamers.

Ingredients

All the various Chinese ingredients you need are widely available these days in most supermarkets and grocery stores. However, some speciality foods and ingredients may only be found in Chinese and Asian supermarkets or from online suppliers.

Bamboo shoots

Fresh bamboo shoots have a distinctive taste, but are difficult to obtain. Canned sliced bamboo shoots are widely available and have a sweet flavor and crunchy texture.

Bitter melon

This unusual-looking vegetable has a bumpy green skin and a slightly bitter taste, and is valued for its medicinal qualities.

Fermented black beans

Also known as salted beans or preserved beans, these small black soybeans have a distinctive salty taste and rich aroma, and are used as a seasoning, usually with ginger, garlic, and chile. You can buy them in jars or cans.

Chili bean paste

This is made from a mixture of ground chiles, salt, garlic, and oil that has been fermented to form a rich paste, and is used as a seasoning in Chinese dishes.

Chili sauce

Made from chiles, vinegar, sugar, and salt, this bright red sauce is sometimes used in Chinese cooking but mainly as a dipping sauce or to add heat to any dish.

Chinese rice wine

This amber-colored matured rice wine, also known as Shaoxing rice wine, is widely used in Chinese cooking. A dry pale sherry can be substituted for it in any of the recipes.

Chinese sausage (lap chong)

These thin sausages, about 6 inches in length, are made from cured duck liver, pork liver, or pork. They are used to season rice and poultry dishes, and they must be cooked before being eaten.

Cinnamon

In Chinese cooking, the cinnamon bark's aromatic flavor is widely used in braised dishes and is one of the ingredients in Chinese five-spice powder.

Dried Chinese mushrooms

Dried Chinese mushrooms need to be rehydrated in hot water before using. They have an intense meaty flavor and the soaking liquid is often used in place of stock in a sauce. The flesh is usually finely chopped and sautéed in Chinese vegetable dishes.

Hoisin sauce

Part of the bean sauce family, this rich, thick and dark sauce is made from soybean paste, garlic, vinegar, sugar, and spices.

Noodles

Three main types of noodles are used:

Egg noodles are made from wheat flour and eggs, and they are available fresh and dried. They come in different thicknesses and are usually yellowish in color. They are used in stir-fries as well as soups.

Rice noodles are made from rice flour, wheat starch, and water, and they are available fresh and dried.

Cellophane noodles (also known as transparent or bean thread noodles) are made from ground mung beans. They are available dried and are fine and white in color. Once soaked, they become soft and translucent.

Oyster sauce

This popular southern Chinese sauce is thick and brown with a rich taste. Made from oysters, soy sauce, and spices, it is highly versatile and adds a boost of flavor to many dishes.

Preserved cabbage

Cabbage leaves are pickled in a mixture of salt, vinegar, and sugar, and they are used as a seasoning. Preserved cabbage is available in cans and should always be rinsed before using.

Rice

Long-grain rice is the most popular type of rice in Chinese cooking and there are many different varieties.

Rice vinegar

Used widely in Chinese cooking and made from rice and grains, rice vinegar has a sweet, tart, and slightly pungent flavor. Black rice vinegar is dark in color and is used in braised dishes and sauces.

Sesame oil

A highly aromatic oil made from sesame seeds, this is used as a flavoring in small quantities in many Chinese dishes.

Sichuan or Szechuan peppercorns

These are dried berries from a shrub, and have a sharp, slightly numbing effect on the tongue with a clean lemony spiciness. They are one of the components of Chinese five-spice powder.

Soy sauce

Used in China more than 3,000 years ago, this sauce is made from fermented soybeans, flour, and water that is distilled. There are two main types of soy sauce: dark and light. Light soy is light in color, full of flavor, and widely used in Chinese cooking. It is slightly saltier than dark soy sauce. Dark soy sauce is aged for longer than the light type and is thicker and darker.

Spring roll wrappers

These paper-thin pastry dough skins made from flour and water are used for making spring rolls and are about 6 inches square. They can be bought already made, frozen in packages, and need to be thawed before using.

Star anise

This star-shaped, aromatic licorice-flavored seed pod is widely used in braising, imparting a rich fragrance. It is also an ingredient in Chinese five-spice powder.

Tofu

Also known as doufu or soybean curd, tofu plays an important part in Chinese cooking. It is highly nutritious, rich in protein, and very low in saturated fats. It is easy to digest, inexpensive, and versatile. Made from yellow soybeans, tofu is usually sold in two main forms, firm and silken.

Water chestnuts

Fresh water chestnuts add crunch and texture to many Chinese dishes, but they are difficult to obtain. Canned water chestnuts, however, are widely available.

Wonton wrappers

Made from egg and flour, these wrappers are used for dim sum, wontons, and dumplings, and they are available fresh or frozen. They are sold in packages and are about 3 inches square. If frozen, defrost before using.

Yellow bean sauce

Also known as bean sauce, this thick, spicy fermented sauce is made from yellow beans, flour, and salt. It adds spicy–aromatic flavor to dishes and is available in jars in Chinese supermarkets.

Getting started

Don't be hampered by the misconception that Chinese food is difficult to prepare at home. It really doesn't demand any more skill, effort, or time than any other type of cooking. As long as you have a few key staple ingredients and a large wok or nonstick skillet, you can cook most dishes in this book. Many of the recipes in this book take less than 20 minutes to cook, and a big plus point is that you can do a lot of the preparation ahead of time, such as chopping the vegetables, which makes it so much quicker and easier when it comes to cooking the dish.

By buying this book, you have decided to take the plunge and start cooking healthy Chinese food. Congratulations! All the recipes in this book have been specially selected as being low in fat. Prepared properly, Chinese food can be beneficial to your whole well-being, as well as being full of flavor.

soups & appetizers

tofu salad with cilantro

Serves **4**

Preparation time **10 minutes**, plus standing

1 lb **firm tofu**, drained

6 **scallions**, finely shredded

⅔ cup coarsely chopped **cilantro leaves**

1 large **mild red chile,** seeded and finely sliced

¼ cup **light soy sauce**

2 teaspoons **sesame oil**

Cut the tofu into bite-size cubes and carefully arrange on a serving plate in a single layer. Sprinkle with the scallions, cilantro, and chile.

Drizzle the soy sauce and oil the tofu, then let stand at room temperature for 10 minutes before serving.

For steamed chile tofu, drain 1 lb firm tofu, cut it into cubes, and put it onto a heatproof plate that will fit inside a bamboo steamer. Cover and steam over a wok or large saucepan of boiling water (see page 14) for 20 minutes, then drain off the excess water and carefully transfer to a serving plate. Heat ¼ cup light soy sauce, 1 tablespoon each sesame oil and peanut oil, and 2 teaspoons oyster sauce in a small saucepan until hot. Pour the sauce over the tofu, sprinkle with 4 thinly sliced scallions, 1 finely chopped red chile, and a small handful of finely chopped cilantro leaves, and serve.

winter cabbage & ginger soup

Serves **4**

Preparation time **10 minutes**

Cooking time **15 minutes**

5 cups boiling **chicken stock**
   or **vegetable stock**

5½ cups coarsely chopped
   napa cabbage

2 tablespoons peeled and
   finely chopped **fresh
   ginger root**

2 **star anise**

2 tablespoons **light soy sauce**

½ teaspoon **sesame oil**

white pepper

Put the stock into a large saucepan and bring to a boil.

Add the cabbage, ginger, and star anise to the stock,
return to a boil, and cook for 10–12 minutes.

Remove from the heat and stir in the soy sauce and
oil, season with white pepper, and ladle into warm
bowls to serve.

For stir-fried napa cabbage with ginger & garlic,
remove and discard the outer leaves from ½ napa
cabbage and cut into large pieces. Pound 3 garlic
cloves with a large pinch of salt in a mortar with a pestle
until coarsely ground. Heat a wok or large, nonstick
skillet over high heat, add 2 tablespoons peanut oil,
and heat until almost smoking. Add the garlic and
1 tablespoon peeled and grated fresh ginger root,
then immediately add the cabbage and stir-fry, moving
the pan contents constantly to prevent the garlic from
burning. Cook until the cabbage is heated through
but still crunchy. Transfer to a warm serving plate and
season with white pepper before serving.

salmon & spinach dim sum

Makes **28**
Preparation time **30 minutes**,
  plus cooling
Cooking time **20 minutes**

low-calorie cooking spray
1 **carrot**, finely diced
1 tablespoon peeled and finely
  chopped **fresh ginger root**
1 **garlic clove**, crushed
4 **scallions**, finely chopped
½ teaspoon **sesame oil**
2 cups finely shredded
  baby spinach leaves
8 oz piece of skinless
  salmon fillet
1 **egg white**
2 tablespoons **cornstarch**
28 **fresh wonton wrappers**
¼ cup **Chinese rice wine**
¼ cup **light soy sauce**
salt

Spray a nonstick skillet with cooking spray and heat over medium heat. Add the carrot, ginger, garlic, and scallions and cook, stirring, for 5 minutes. Stir in the sesame oil and spinach and cook for a few seconds until the spinach has wilted. Increase the heat and cook for 1 minute, until any liquid has evaporated. Let cool.

Puree the salmon in a food processor. Whisk the egg white with the cornstarch in a large bowl, then add the salmon, the vegetable mixture, and salt to taste and mix thoroughly.

Spoon 1 teaspoon of the fish mixture in the center of a wonton wrapper. Dampen the wrapper edges with water and bring up the sides around the filling. Pinch the the top to seal. Repeat with the remaining wrappers and fish mixture. (You can refrigerate, covered with plastic wrap, for up to 12 hours before cooking.)

Place without touching in a stacking bamboo steamer lined with nonstick parchment paper, cover, and steam (see page 14) for 8–10 minutes, until cooked through. If you don't have stacking baskets, steam in 2 batches and keep the cooked batch hot over a saucepan of simmering water while cooking the second batch.

Meanwhile, mix together the rice wine and soy sauce in a small bowl and serve with the dim sum.

For sweet chili dipping sauce, put 1 seeded and chopped red bell pepper, 2 halved red chiles, ½ cup granulated sugar, and ½ cup each of rice vinegar and cold water in a saucepan. Bring to a boil, then simmer for 30 minutes, until it turns pinkish. Cool, then process in a blender until smooth. Return to the pan and simmer for 20 minutes, until slightly sticky. Cool and serve.

mushroom & ginger wontons

Serves **4**

Preparation time **30 minutes**, plus cooling

Cooking time **10–12 minutes**

2 tablespoons **vegetable oil**
1 **garlic clove**, crushed
1 teaspoon peeled and grated **fresh ginger root**
8 oz **mixed mushrooms**, trimmed and finely chopped
1 tablespoon **dark soy sauce**
1 tablespoon chopped **cilantro**
16 **fresh wonton wrappers**
salt and **black pepper**

Dressing
1 teaspoon **dried red pepper flakes**
⅔ cup **vegetable stock**
1 tablespoon **rice vinegar**
1 tablespoon **light soy sauce**
2 teaspoons **granulated sugar**
¼ teaspoon freshly ground **Sichuan pepper**

Heat the oil in a skillet over medium heat, add the garlic and ginger, and stir-fry for 2–3 minutes. Add the mushrooms and soy sauce and cook, stirring, for 3–4 minutes, until golden. Remove from the heat, season to taste with salt and black pepper, and stir in the cilantro. Let cool.

Meanwhile, put all the ingredients for the dressing into a saucepan and heat over low heat, stirring, until hot but not boiling. Keep warm.

Lay a wonton wrapper in the palm of one hand. Place 1 teaspoon of the mushroom mixture in the center. Dampen the wrapper edges with water, then fold the wrapper in half diagonally and press the edges together to seal and form a package. (You can refrigerate, covered with plastic wrap, for up to 12 hours before cooking.)

Bring a large saucepan of lightly salted water to a rolling boil, add the wontons, and cook for 2–3 minutes, until they rise to the surface. Gently drain and transfer to warm bowls. Strain the dressing over and serve.

For crispy mushroom wontons, heat 2 inches vegetable oil in a wok or deep, heavy saucepan until it reaches 350–375°F, or until a cube of bread browns in 30 seconds. Add the wontons, in batches, and deep-fry for 2–3 minutes, until crisp and golden. Remove with a slotted spoon and drain on paper towels. Serve with Sweet Chili Dipping Sauce (see page 26).

chicken noodle soup

Serves **4**

Preparation time **10 minutes**, plus cooling

Cooking time **40 minutes**

2 **chicken quarters**, about 1½ lb in total

1 **onion**, chopped

4 **garlic cloves**, chopped

3 slices of **fresh ginger root**, peeled and bruised

8½ cups **cold water**

4 oz **dried fine egg noodles**

2 tablespoons **light soy sauce**

1 **fresh red Thai chile,** seeded and sliced

2 **scallions**, sliced

2 tablespoons **cilantro leaves**

salt and **black pepper**

Put the chicken quarters, onion, garlic, ginger, measured water, and salt and black pepper to taste in a saucepan. Bring to a boil, then reduce the heat and simmer gently, uncovered, for 30 minutes, skimming off any scum that rises to the surface.

Remove the chicken, strain the stock, and let cool. Meanwhile, when cool enough to handle, skin the chicken and shred the flesh.

Cook the noodles in a saucepan of boiling water according to the package directions, until just tender. Drain well and divide among 4 warm bowls.

Heat the reserved stock in a saucepan with the soy sauce. Add the chicken and simmer for 5 minutes.

Spoon the stock and chicken over the noodles and sprinkle with the chile, scallion, and cilantro leaves. Serve immediately.

For aromatic chicken noodle soup, cook the chicken quarters with the other ingredients in the water as above, adding 6 large, torn kaffir lime leaves. Remove the chicken and strain the stock, then skin the chicken and shred as above. Heat the stock in a saucepan with 2 tablespoons Thai fish sauce, juice of ½ lime, 2 teaspoons sugar, and 1 seeded and sliced red Thai chile. Add the chicken and simmer for 5 minutes. Meanwhile, put 4 oz dried rice noodles in a heatproof bowl, pour over enough boiling water to cover, and let sit for 5 minutes, or prepare according to package directions, until just tender, then drain. Serve the noodles topped with the stock and chicken, garnished with sliced chiles, cilantro, and shredded kaffir lime leaves.

black tea & star anise eggs

Serves **4**

Preparation time **10 minutes**,
  plus cooling and standing

Cooking time **2¼ hours**

8 **eggs**

3¼ cups **water**

1 tablespoon **light soy sauce**

1 tablespoon **dark soy sauce**

2 tablespoons **black tea
  leaves**

2 **star anise**

1 **cinnamon stick**

1 tablespoon finely grated
  orange zest

salt

crisp lettuce leaves, to serve

Put the eggs into a large saucepan with 1 teaspoon salt and cover with cold water. Bring to a boil, then reduce the heat and simmer for 12 minutes. Remove from the heat, drain, and let cool. When cool, tap the eggs with the back of a spoon to crack the shells all over, but don't remove the shells.

Combine the measured water, soy sauces, ¼ teaspoon salt, tea leaves, star anise, cinnamon stick, and orange zest in a large saucepan. Bring to a boil, then reduce the heat, cover, and simmer for 2 hours. Remove from the heat, add the eggs, and let stand for at least 8–12 hours.

Shell the eggs and cut in half, then serve with crisp lettuce leaves.

For Chinese-style open egg omelet, spray a nonstick ovenproof skillet with low-calorie cooking spray and heat over high heat. Add 6 sliced scallions, 2 chopped garlic cloves, and 1 finely chopped seeded red chile and stir-fry for 1–2 minutes. Add 1 tablespoon each of oyster sauce, light soy sauce, and sweet chili sauce and cook, stirring, for 1–2 minutes. Beat together 6 eggs in a bowl and stir in ¼ cup chopped cilantro leaves. Season with salt and black pepper and pour into the pan. Cook over medium heat for about 10–12 minutes, or until the underside is starting to set. Transfer the pan to a preheated medium-high broiler and cook for 4–5 minutes, or until the top is set and golden. Remove from the broiler and serve warm or at room temperature.

spinach, mushroom & tofu broth

Serves **4**

Preparation time **20 minutes**,
 plus soaking

Cooking time **10 minutes**

4 **dried Chinese mushrooms**

8 large fresh **shiitake
 mushrooms**

low-calorie cooking spray

2 **garlic cloves**, finely chopped

¼ teaspoon **chili paste**

1 teaspoon **Chinese rice wine**

5 cups boiling **vegetable
 stock**

1 teaspoon **light soy sauce**

½ teaspoon **granulated sugar**

1 tablespoon **cornstarch**,
 mixed to a paste with
 2 tablespoons **cold water**

12 oz **firm tofu**, drained and
 cut into bite-size cubes

1 (12 oz) package **baby
 spinach leaves**

½ teaspoon **sesame oil**

black pepper

Put the dried mushrooms into a heatproof bowl, pour over enough boiling water to cover, and let soak for 30 minutes, until softened. Drain and squeeze out the excess water. Remove and discard the stems, and thinly slice the caps. Trim and then thinly slice the fresh mushrooms.

Spray a nonstick wok or skillet with cooking spray and heat over medium-high heat. Add the garlic and chili paste and stir-fry for a few seconds, until aromatic. Add the mushrooms and stir-fry for 2 minutes.

Stir the rice wine into the pan, followed by the stock, soy sauce, sugar, and cornstarch paste. Season to taste with black pepper. Bring to a boil, stirring constantly, then stir in the tofu and spinach. Return to a boil and cook, stirring, for 2–3 minutes, until the spinach turns bright green and the mixture has thickened.

Remove the pan from the heat and stir in the sesame oil. Ladle into warm bowls and serve immediately.

For spinach, tomato & tofu salad, put 4 cups baby spinach leaves in a salad bowl with 3 cups halved cherry tomatoes and 12 oz firm tofu, drained and cut into bite-size cubes. Mix together 2 tablespoons each of light soy sauce and sweet chili sauce, 1 tablespoon sesame oil ,and 1 teaspoon each of peeled and grated fresh ginger root and garlic and chili paste in a small bowl, and season with salt and black pepper. Drizzle the dressing over the salad ingredients in the bowl. Toss gently to mix before serving.

bang bang chicken noodle salad

Serves **4**

Preparation time **15 minutes**,
 plus standing

8 oz **dried fine rice vermicelli noodles**

4 cooked boneless **chicken breasts**, skinned and coarsely shredded

1 **cucumber**, halved, seeded, and cut into matchsticks

8 **scallions**, thinly sliced

1 **red chile,** thinly sliced

1/3 cup **reduced-fat smooth peanut butter**

1/3 cup **light soy sauce**

2 tablespoons **white wine vinegar**

1 tablespoon **honey**

1 teaspoon **sesame oil**

1 teaspoon **chili oil**

1/3 cup **warm water**

2 tablespoons **sesame seeds**, toasted

Put the noodles into a large heatproof bowl, pour over enough boiling hot water to cover, and let stand for 10 minutes, or prepare according to the package directions, until just tender. Drain and return to the bowl. Add the chicken, cucumber, scallions, and chile, and toss to combine. Transfer to a serving bowl.

Stir together the peanut butter, soy sauce, vinegar, honey, oils, and 2 tablespoons of the measured water in a bowl until well combined. Gradually add the remaining water to the sauce, stirring, until the sauce reaches pouring consistency.

Drizzle the sauce over the salad. Sprinkle with the sesame seeds and serve.

For chicken, shrimp & lemon grass with noodles,

spray a large, nonstick wok or skillet with low-calorie cooking spray and heat over high heat. Add 1 lb ground chicken, 1 teaspoon each of peeled and finely grated fresh ginger root and garlic, 1 finely chopped red chile, and 1 tablespoon lemon grass paste and stir-fry, breaking up the chicken with a wooden spoon, for 3–4 minutes, until the chicken is browned. Stir in 10 oz cooked peeled shrimp and 1 tablespoon each of light soy sauce and Thai fish sauce and cook briefly, stirring, until heated through. Serve immediately with the noodles.

sichuan pickled cucumber

Serves **4**

Preparation time **10 minutes**, plus marinating

2 **cucumbers**

1 teaspoon **dried red pepper flakes**

2 **scallions**, finely chopped

1 **garlic clove**, crushed

½ teaspoon packed **light brown sugar**

5 teaspoons **light soy sauce**

2 teaspoons **sesame oil**

2 teaspoons **chili oil**

¼ teaspoon **black rice vinegar**

½ teaspoon **sesame seeds**, toasted

Cut the cucumbers into finger-thick batons and put into a wide glass or ceramic bowl.

Mix together all the remaining ingredients in a small bowl and pour them over the cucumber. Toss to mix well. Cover and let marinate at room temperature for 1 hour.

Spoon onto small plates and serve with rice.

For Sichuan stir-fried cucumbers with hot chili oil,
seed and thinly slice 3 large cucumbers into thin batons. Heat 2 tablespoons peanut oil in a large, nonstick wok or skillet until smoking. Add 1 tablespoon crushed Sichuan peppercorns and the cucumber and stir-fry for 1–2 minutes. Drizzle in 2 tablespoons light soy sauce and cook, stirring, for 30–40 seconds. Remove from the heat and drizzle 2 tablespoons chili oil over the top. Serve immediately with rice.

peanut, squid & noodle salad

Serves **4**

Preparation time **25 minutes**, plus standing

Cooking time **15 minutes**

6 oz **dried fine rice noodles**

1 lb cleaned **baby squid**

3 **red chiles**, seeded and finely chopped

3 **garlic cloves**, finely chopped

2 tablespoons chopped **cilantro**, plus extra leaves to serve

3 tablespoons **peanut oil**

1¼ cups coarsely chopped **unsalted peanuts**

1 cup coarsely chopped **green beans**

3 tablespoons **Thai fish sauce**

1 teaspoon **granulated sugar**

3 tablespoons **lemon juice**

3 tablespoons **water**

Put the noodles into a large heatproof bowl, pour over enough boiling hot water to cover, and let stand for 5–8 minutes, or prepare according to the package directions, until just tender. Drain well and rinse under cold running water.

Cut the squid bodies in half lengthwise and use a sharp knife to make a series of slashes in a diagonal crisscross pattern on the underside of each piece.

Mix together the chiles, garlic, and chopped cilantro in a glass or ceramic bowl. Add the squid pieces and toss in the mixture, then let stand for about 20 minutes.

Heat the oil in a nonstick wok or large skillet over medium heat. Add the peanuts and stir-fry for about 2–3 minutes, until golden brown. Remove with a slotted spoon and set aside. Add the squid to the pan and stir-fry for 2–3 minutes, or until beginning to curl and turn white. Set aside with the peanuts.

Add the green beans to the pan and stir-fry for 2 minutes. Stir in the Thai fish sauce, sugar, lemon juice, and measured water and cook for another minute. Remove the pan from the heat, add the drained noodles, and toss together. Add the peanuts, squid, and extra cilantro leaves and toss again. Serve warm or cool with lime wedges, if desired.

spicy sui mai dumplings

Makes **36**
Preparation time **30 minutes**
Cooking time **6–8 minutes**

5 oz **ground pork**
4 oz **raw peeled jumbo shrimp**, very finely chopped
2 **scallions,** finely chopped
1 **red chile,** finely chopped
2 **garlic cloves,** crushed
2 teaspoons peeled and finely grated **fresh ginger root**
2 tablespoons **oyster sauce**
1 teaspoon **sesame oil**
5 canned **water chestnuts,** rinsed, drained and finely chopped
36 **fresh wonton wrappers**

Dipping sauce
2 tablespoons **dark soy sauce**
2 tablespoons **Chinese rice wine**
2 teaspoons peeled and finely chopped **fresh ginger root**
1 **red chile,** finely chopped

Mix together the pork, shrimp, scallions, chile, garlic, ginger, oyster sauce, sesame oil, and water chestnuts with your fingers in a bowl until well combined.

Lay a wonton wrapper in the palm of one hand. Place 1 teaspoonful of the pork mixture in the center. Dampen the wrapper edges with water and bring up the sides, then press them around the filling, leaving the filling exposed. Gently tap on the work surface to create a flat bottom. Repeat with the remaining wrappers and pork mixture. (You can refrigerate on a tray lined with nonstick parchment paper for up to 1 hour before cooking.)

Combine all the ingredients for the sauce in a small bowl.

Place the dumplings without touching in stacking bamboo steamer baskets lined with nonstick parchment paper, cover, and steam over a wok or large saucepan of boiling water (see page 14) for 6–8 minutes, until cooked through. If you don't have stacking baskets, steam in 2 batches. Transfer the cooked batch to a heatproof plate, cover loosely with aluminum foil, and keep hot over a saucepan of simmering water while cooking the second batch.

Serve the dumplings with the sauce for dipping.

For shrimp & chive dumplings, follow the recipe above to prepare the filling mixture, omitting the ground pork, using 10 oz raw, peeled jumbo shrimp and replacing the red chile with 1 tablespoon minced garlic chives. Make the dumplings and steam until cooked through as above, then serve with homemade Sweet Chili Dipping Sauce (see page 26).

chili crab on noodle nests

Makes **20**
Preparation time **10 minutes**,
   plus cooling
Cooking time **15 minutes**

4 oz **fresh fine egg noodles**
1 tablespoon **sunflower oil**,
   plus extra for greasing and
   brushing
2 **scallions**, thinly sliced
2 **garlic cloves**, finely chopped
1 teaspoon peeled and finely
   chopped **fresh ginger root**
1 **red chile,** seeded and finely
   chopped
8 oz **fresh white crabmeat**
2 tablespoons **sweet chili
   sauce**
¼ cup finely chopped **cilantro**

Grease 20 cups in 1–2 nonstick mini tart pans lightly with oil. Divide the noodles into 20 portions and press each portion into a tart cup to form a tart shape, making sure the bottom is covered. Lightly brush with more oil and bake in a preheated oven, at 350°F, for 8–10 minutes, or until crisp and firm. Remove from the cups and let cool on a wire rack.

Heat the 1 tablespoon oil in a large, nonstick wok or skillet, add the scallions, garlic, ginger, and chile and stir-fry for 2–3 minutes. Add the crabmeat and stir-fry for another 1–2 minutes, then remove from the heat, stir in the sweet chili sauce and cilantro, and toss to mix well.

Place 1 heaping teaspoon of the chili crab mixture into each cooled noodle nest and serve immediately.

For chili crab linguine, cook 12 oz dried linguine in a large saucepan of lightly salted boiling water for about 10 minutes, or according to the package directions, then drain. Meanwhile, heat 2 tablespoons olive oil in a large skillet, add 1 finely chopped large red chile, and stir-fry for 2 minutes. Stir in 4 thinly sliced scallions, 12 oz fresh white crabmeat, the juice of 1 lime, and 2 tablespoons coarsely chopped cilantro leaves and warm through. Add the drained linguine and toss all the ingredients together. Dress the crab linguine with 2 tablespoons olive oil and serve immediately.

hot & sour soup with tofu

Serves **4**
Preparation time **20 minutes**
Cooking time **25 minutes**

5 cups **vegetable stock**
   or **chicken stock**
10 oz **mixed mushrooms**,
   trimmed and sliced
⅓ cup canned sliced **bamboo
   shoots**, rinsed and drained
1 teaspoon peeled and grated
   fresh ginger root
2 **garlic cloves,** crushed
1 tablespoon **soy sauce**
¼ teaspoon **dried red
   pepper flakes**
1 tablespoon **cornstarch**
3 tablespoons **white wine
   vinegar**
1 **egg**, beaten
4 **scallions**, chopped
small handful of chopped
   cilantro
7 oz **firm tofu**, drained and cut
   into bite-size cubes

To garnish
shredded **scallions**
thinly sliced **red chile**

Combine the stock, mushrooms, bamboo shoots, ginger, garlic, soy sauce, and red pepper flakes in a saucepan. Bring to a boil, then reduce the heat to low, cover, and simmer for about 15 minutes while you assemble the rest of the ingredients.

Mix the cornstarch with the vinegar in a small bowl until smooth, then set aside.

Return the soup to a rolling boil. Drizzle in the beaten egg while stirring slowly to create long strands. Stir in the scallions, cilantro, and cornstarch mixture. Reduce the heat and simmer, stirring occcaisonally, for about 3 minutes, until the stock has thickened slightly.

Stir in the tofu and cook briefly until heated through. Serve the soup garnished with shredded scallions and red chile slices.

For hot tofu & scallion stir-fry, spray a nonstick wok or large skillet with low-calorie cooking spray and heat over high heat. Add 3 crushed garlic cloves and 1 teaspoon peeled and grated fresh ginger root and stir-fry for 10–20 seconds, then add 12 thickly sliced scallions, 1 lb firm tofu, drained and cut into bite-size cubes, and 1 diced red chile. Stir-fry for 4–5 minutes, until the tofu is lightly browned. Add ½ cup vegetable stock and 2 tablespoons dark soy sauce and cook over medium heat for 6–8 minutes, until all the liquid is absorbed. Serve immediately with egg noodles or rice.

pot sticker dumplings

Serves **4**
Preparation time **40 minutes**,
   plus resting
Cooking time **20 minutes**

1 tablespoon **peanut oil**
½ cup **boiling water**
sweet chili dipping sauce
   (see page 26), to serve

Dumpling dough
1¼ cups **all-purpose flour**,
   plus extra for dusting
½ cup **boiling water**

Filling
2 oz **raw peeled jumbo
   shrimp**, finely chopped
2 oz **ground pork**
4 **scallions**, minced
1 teaspoon peeled and
   grated **fresh ginger root**
½ tablespoon **Chinese
   rice wine**
1 tablespoon **dark soy sauce**,
   plus extra to serve
¼ teaspoon ground **white
   pepper**

Put the flour for the dough in a mixing bowl and, using a fork, gradually stir in the measured water until incorporated. Add more water if the mixture seems dry.

Knead the dough on a work surface for 8–10 minutes, dusting with a little flour if sticky. Return to the bowl, cover with a damp dish towel, and let rest for 20 minutes.

Mix together all the ingredients for the filling in a separate bowl until well combined. Set aside.

Knead the dough again for 5–6 minutes, until smooth, then shape into a roll about 9 inches long and 1 inch in diameter, then slice into 16 pieces. Roll each piece into a small ball, then roll out each ball into a 3½ inch "pancake." Cover with a damp dish towel to prevent them from drying out. Place 2 teaspoons of filling in the center of each pancake and moisten the edges with water. Fold the dough in half to form a semicircle and pinch the edges together with your fingers. Pleat around the edge, pinching to seal well.

Heat the peanut oil in a large, lidded nonstick skillet until hot and add the dumplings. Reduce the heat and cook for 2 minutes, until lightly browned. Add the measured water, cover the pan, and simmer gently for 12–15 minutes, or until most of the liquid is absorbed. Check halfway through and add more water, if necessary. Uncover and cook for another 2–3 minutes. Serve with dark soy sauce and sweet chili sauce for dipping.

For chili beef pot sticker dumplings, prepare the dumpling dough as above. For the filling, replace the shrimp and pork with 4 oz ground beef and add 2 finely chopped red chiles. Continue as above.

baked vegetable spring rolls

Serves **4**

Preparation time **25 minutes**,
  plus soaking and cooling

Cooking time **15–20 minutes**

16 **dried Chinese mushrooms**

low-calorie cooking spray

1 tablespoon **light soy sauce**

2 teaspoons **Chinese five-
  spice powder**

1 cup **bean sprouts**

4 **scallions**, finely chopped

1 small **carrot**, finely chopped

1 teaspoon peeled and grated
  fresh ginger root

2 tablespoons **oyster sauce**

16 **spring roll wrappers**,
  thawed if frozen

1 tablespoon **cornstarch**,
  mixed to a paste with
  2 tablespoons **cold water**

1 **egg yolk**, beaten

salt and **white pepper**

sweet chili dipping sauce
  (see page 26), to serve

Put the dried mushrooms into a heatproof bowl, pour over boiling water to cover and let soak for 30 minutes, until softened. Drain and squeeze out the excess water. Remove and discard the stems, and finely chop the caps.

Spray a large wok or skillet with cooking spray and heat until smoking. Add the mushrooms and stir-fry for 1–2 minutes, then stir in the soy sauce and five-spice powder. Remove from the pan and let cool for 10 minutes. Wipe the pan clean with paper towels.

Put the bean sprouts, scallions, carrot, and ginger into a bowl, add the mushroom mixture and oyster sauce, and season well with salt and white pepper. Mix well.

Lay 2 spring roll wrappers on top of each other. Spoon 2 tablespoons of the filling in the center. Brush each corner with cornstarch paste. Fold 2 opposite corners over the filling, then roll the wrapper up tightly from one of the other corners. Seal the roll with a little beaten egg yolk. Repeat with the remaining wrappers and filling.

Arrange the rolls on a baking sheet lined with nonstick parchment paper, lightly spray with cooking spray, and bake in a preheated oven, at 400°F, for 12–15 minutes, or until lightly golden and crisp. Serve immediately with sweet chili sauce for dipping.

For mushroom & bean sprout stir-fry, spray a large, nonstick wok with cooking spray and heat over high heat. Add 12 oz sliced shiitake mushrooms and 1 teaspoon each of grated fresh ginger root and garlic, and stir-fry for 6–8 minutes. Add 1 finely chopped carrot, 6 sliced scallions, and 1 cup bean sprouts and stir-fry for another 3–4 minutes before serving.

egg drop soup

Serves **4**
Preparation time **10 minutes**
Cooking time **10 minutes**

5 cups **chicken stock**
2 tablespoons **cornstarch**
   mixed to a paste with
   3 tablespoons **cold water**
2 tablespoons **dark soy sauce**
1 tablespoon **white wine
   vinegar**
6 **scallions**, thinly sliced
3 **eggs**, beaten
chili oil, for drizzling
sliced scallions,
   to garnish

Put the stock into a saucepan and bring to a boil.

Stir the cornstarch and water mixture into the stock. Add the soy sauce, vinegar, and scallions. Return to a boil, then reduce the heat and simmer, stirring occasionally, for about 3 minutes, until the stock has thickened slightly.

Pour the beaten eggs gradually into the soup while stirring vigorously until just set in strands.

Remove the pan from the heat, ladle the soup into warm bowls, drizzle with chili oil, and serve.

For shrimp & garlic chive soup, bring 5 cups fish stock to a boil in a saucepan. Mix 2 tablespoons cornstarch to a paste with 3 tablespoons cold water, then stir into the stock. Stir in 2 tablespoons light soy sauce, a handful of finely chopped garlic chives, 12 oz raw, peeled jumbo shrimp, and 2 thinly sliced scallions. Return to a boil, then simmer, stirring occasionally, for about 5 minutes, until the mixture has thickened slightly and the shrimp have turned pink and are firm. Gradually pour in 2 beaten eggs while stirring vigorously until just set in strands. Remove the pan from the heat, ladle the soup into warm bowls, and serve immediately.

crayfish rolls with hoisin sauce

Serves **4**

Preparation time **25 minutes**,
   plus soaking

Cooking time **1 minute**

8 **rice paper sheets**

16 **long chives**

4 **iceberg lettuce leaves**,
   finely shredded

4 **scallions**, finely shredded
   into matchsticks

16 **mint leaves**, shredded

16 **cooked, peeled
   crayfish tails**

3 tablespoons **hoisin sauce**,
   to serve

Fill a shallow bowl with hot water and soak the rice paper sheets for about 5 minutes, until softened. Remove the sheets from the water and place on a clean, dry dish towel. Cut in half.

Blanch the chives in a saucepan of boiling water for 10 seconds, then drain and cool under cold running water.

Lay 1 half-sheet of rice paper on a clean work surface and fill with a little lettuce, scallions, mint, and a crayfish tail. Roll up the rice paper sheet to enclose the ingredients, folding in the ends as you work. Tie a chive around the center of the roll to seal it closed, then put onto a tray and cover with a clean, damp dish towel while making the remaining rolls.

Serve the crayfish rolls with the hoisin sauce for dipping.

For shrimp & bamboo shoot spring rolls, brush 1 sheet of phyllo pastry with a little melted butter. With the short side of the pastry in line with your body, place 1 raw, peeled jumbo shrimp and a small pile of canned bamboo shoots, rinsed and drained, in the center of the pastry at the edge. Roll up the phyllo pastry sheet to enclose the ingredients, folding in the ends as you work. Repeat with 15 more sheets of phyllo pastry, 15 more shrimp, and some bamboo shoots. Brush the spring rolls with melted butter and bake in a preheated oven, at 350°F, for 10–15 minutes, until golden brown. Serve with hoisin sauce for dipping.

shrimp & pork wonton soup

Serves **4**
Preparation time **25 minutes**
Cooking time **5–6 minutes**

4 oz **ground pork**
5 oz **raw, peeled shrimp**
4 **scallions**, finely chopped
1 **garlic clove**, peeled
½ inch piece of **fresh ginger root**, chopped
1 tablespoon **oyster sauce**
20 **fresh wonton wrappers**
3¼ cups **chicken stock**
1 head of **Chinese greens**, shredded
1–2 tablespoons **Thai fish sauce**

To serve
leaves from a small bunch of **cilantro**
1 tablespoon **sesame seeds**

Put the pork, shrimp, 2 of the scallions, the garlic, ginger, and oyster sauce into a food processor and process to a paste.

Spoon 1 teaspoon of the pork mixture in the center of a wonton wrapper. Dampen the edges with water, bring up the sides around the filling, and pinch the edges together to seal. Repeat with the remaining wrappers and pork mixture. (You can refrigerate, covered with plastic wrap, for up to 12 hours before cooking.)

Bring the stock to a boil in a large saucepan, then reduce the heat, add the wontons, and simmer for 4–5 minutes. Remove a wonton and check that it has become firm, which will indicate that it is cooked.

Add the Chinese greens to the pan and cook for 1 minute. Season the stock with the Thai fish sauce. Divide the soup among 4 warm bowls and serve with a few cilantro leaves and a sprinkling of sesame seeds.

For sesame wontons with soy dipping sauce, follow the recipe above to make the wontons. Place without touching in stacking bamboo steamer baskets lined with parchment paper, cover, and steam (see page 14) for 5 minutes, until cooked through. If you don't have stacking baskets, steam in 2 batches and keep the cooked batch hot over a saucepan of simmering water while cooking the second batch. Meanwhile, make a dipping sauce by mixing together 3 tablespoons light soy sauce, 2 teaspoons grated fresh ginger root, 1 thinly sliced red chile, and 1 tablespoon Thai fish sauce in a small bowl. Sprinkle 2 tablespoons sesame seeds over the wontons and serve with the dipping sauce.

black bean soup with soba

Serves **4**

Preparation time **10 minutes**

Cooking time **8 minutes**

8 oz **dried soba noodles**

2 tablespoons **peanut** or **vegetable oil**

1 bunch of **scallions**, sliced

2 **garlic cloves**, coarsely chopped

1 **red chile,** seeded and sliced

1½ inch piece of **fresh ginger root**, peeled and grated

½ cup **black bean sauce** or **black bean stir-fry sauce**

3¼ cups **vegetable stock**

3 cups shredded **bok choy** or **Chinese greens**

2 teaspoons **light soy sauce**

1 teaspoon **granulated sugar**

⅓ cup **raw unsalted peanuts**

Cook the noodles in a large saucepan of boiling water for about 5 minutes, or according to the package directions, until just tender.

Meanwhile, heat the oil in a saucepan over medium heat, add the scallions and garlic, and stir-fry for 1 minute. Add the chile, ginger, black bean sauce, and stock and bring to a boil.

Stir the bok choy or Chinese greens, soy sauce, sugar, and peanuts into the soup, then reduce the heat and simmer gently for 4 minutes.

Drain the noodles, rinse with fresh hot water, and spoon into 4 warm bowls. Ladle the soup over the top and serve immediately.

For chicken & black bean soup, follow the recipe above to cook the noodles. Meanwhile, heat the oil in a saucepan, add 3 boneless, skinless chicken thighs, chopped into small chunks, and cook for 4–5 minutes, or until cooked through. Add the scallions and garlic and continue with the recipe above, replacing the vegetable stock with 3¼ cups chicken stock and omitting the peanuts.

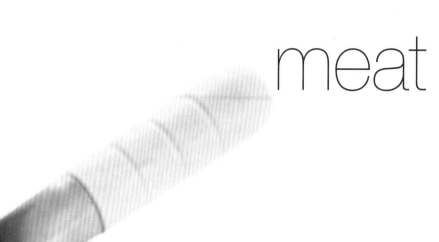

meat

beef & black bean stir-fry

Serves **4**

Preparation time **15 minutes**, plus marinating

Cooking time **15 minutes**

1 cup **black bean sauce**

2 tablespoons **Chinese rice wine**

2 **garlic cloves**, crushed

1 lb lean **tenderloin steak**, thinly sliced

low-calorie cooking spray

1 **onion**, cut into wedges

3 cups **sugar snap peas**

1 **red bell pepper**, cored, seeded, and thinly sliced

Combine the black bean sauce, rice wine, and garlic in a bowl. Put the beef into a glass or ceramic bowl, add half the sauce mixture, and toss to coat evenly. Cover and let marinate in the refrigerator for 3–4 hours.

Spray a nonstick wok or skillet with cooking spray and heat over high heat. Add the steak and stir-fry for 4–5 minutes, or until just cooked. Transfer to a bowl.

Wipe the pan clean with paper towels, respray with cooking spray, and heat over high heat. Add the onion and stir-fry for about 1–2 minutes, until slightly softened. Add the sugar snap peas and red bell pepper and stir-fry for about 2–3 minutes, until just tender.

Return the beef to the pan, add the remaining sauce mixture, and cook, stirring, for about 1 minute, until heated through. Serve with steamed jasmine rice.

For pork, baby mushroom & black bean stir-fry, follow the recipe above, replacing the beef with 1 lb lean pork cutlets, cut into thin strips, and using 3 cups halved baby button mushrooms instead of the sugar snap peas.

roasted char siu pork

Serves **4**

Preparation time **20 minutes**,
plus marinating and resting

Cooking time **45 minutes**

1¼ lb lean **pork tenderloin**

4 **garlic cloves**, crushed

2 tablespoons peeled and
grated **fresh ginger root**

1 teaspoon **Chinese
five-spice powder**

½ cup **light soy sauce**

¼ cup **Chinese rice wine**

3 tablespoons packed **light
brown sugar**

2 tablespoons **hoisin sauce**

2 tablespoons **sweet chili
sauce**

2 tablespoons **honey**

1 tablespoon **peanut oil**

Make deep slashes all over the pork with a sharp knife and put into a shallow glass or ceramic dish. Mix together all the remaining ingredients and spread all over the pork, rubbing it into the slashes. Cover and let marinate in the refrigerator for 3–4 hours, or overnight if time permits.

Put a roasting rack or wire rack over a roasting pan. Pour hot water into the pan to come halfway up the sides. Reserving the marinade, lay the pork on the rack, put the pan into a preheated oven, at 400°F, and roast for 20 minutes.

Turn the pork over and brush well with some of the marinade. Reduce the oven temperature to 350°F and roast for another 20 minutes. Remove from the oven, cover with aluminum foil, and let rest for 10–15 minutes.

Meanwhile, place the remaining marinade in a small saucepan and bring to a boil.

Slice the pork thinly and serve with the extra marinade, together with egg noodles and steamed Chinese greens.

For quick char siu pork fried rice, spray a large, nonstick wok or skillet with low-calorie cooking spray and heat over high heat. Add 2 teaspoons each of finely chopped fresh ginger root and garlic and stir-fry for 30 seconds. Add 1¼ lb lean ground pork and stir-fry for 3–4 minutes. Add ¼ cup Chinese barbecue sauce (char siu sauce), 2 tablespoons light soy sauce, and 1 cup jasmine rice or long-grain rice, freshly cooked and cooled, and toss together for 5–6 minutes, until piping hot. Serve immediately with steamed Chinese greens.

lamb & green bean stir-fry

Serves **4**

Preparation time **15 minutes**

Cooking time **10 minutes**

1 lb boneless lean **lamb cutlets**, cut into 1 inch pieces

3 **garlic cloves**, crushed

1 tablespoon peeled and grated **fresh ginger root**

1 tablespoon **Chinese five-spice powder**

1 teaspoon **dried red pepper flakes**

¼ cup **light soy sauce**

low-calorie cooking spray

1 **onion**, cut into wedges

3 cups trimmed **green beans**

2 tablespoons **kecap manis (Indonesian sweet soy sauce)**

small handful of **mint leaves**

To garnish

chile slivers

cucumber ribbons

Combine the lamb, garlic, ginger, five-spice powder, red pepper flakes, and 2 tablespoons of the soy sauce in a bowl.

Spray a large, nonstick wok or skillet with cooking spray and heat over high heat until just smoking. Add the onion and green beans and stir-fry for about 3–4 minutes, until lightly charred and tender. Transfer to a bowl.

Wipe the pan clean with paper towels, respray with cooking spray, and heat over high heat. Add half the lamb mixture and stir-fry for 2 minutes, or until browned and just cooked through. Transfer to a plate. Wipe the pan clean, spray again with cooking spray, and stir-fry the rest of the lamb mixture in the same way.

Return all the lamb mixture to the pan with the onion mixture and add the remaining soy sauce and the kecap manis. Cook, stirring, for about 30 seconds, until heated through.

Divide among 4 warm bowls, garnish with chile slivers and cucumber ribbons, and serve with egg noodles.

For quick shrimp & green bean stir-fry, follow the recipe above, replacing the lamb with 1 ¼ lb raw, peeled jumbo shrimp. After stir-frying the onion and green beans as above, add the shrimp mixture to the pan and continue to stir-fry for 4–5 minutes, until the shrimp have turned pink and are firm. Remove from the heat and garnish with chopped cilantro before serving with noodles or rice.

broiled hoisin pork

Serves **4**

Preparation time **15 minutes**, plus marinating

Cooking time **10–12 minutes**

8 boneless lean **pork loin cutlets**, about 4 oz each
¼ cup **hoisin sauce**
3 tablespoons **dark soy sauce**
4 **garlic cloves**, crushed
2 teaspoons peeled and finely grated **fresh ginger root**
1 teaspoon **Sichuan peppercorns**, crushed
2 tablespoons **tomato paste**
2 tablespoons **cider vinegar**

To garnish
4 **scallions**, finely shredded
1 **red chile,** seeded and finely shredded

Put the pork cutlets into a shallow glass or ceramic dish in a single layer. Mix together the hoisin sauce, soy sauce, garlic, ginger, crushed Sichuan peppercorns, tomato paste, and vinegar, then brush or spoon the mixture onto the pork. Cover and let marinate in the refrigerator for 2–3 hours.

Arrange the pork on a broiler rack in a single layer and cook under a preheated medium-high broiler for 5–6 minutes on each side, or until cooked through.

Remove from the broiler, garnish with the scallions and red chile, and serve with steamed rice and steamed Chinese greens.

For broiled sweet chili pork chops, put 4 large, lean pork chops, about 6 oz each, into a glass or ceramic dish in a single layer. Mix together ⅓ cup sweet chili sauce, the juice of 1 lime, and 2 teaspoons each of peeled and grated fresh ginger root, garlic, and light soy sauce. Spoon the marinade over the pork chops and toss to coat evenly. Cover and let marinate in the refrigerator for 1–2 hours, or overnight if time permits. Arrange the chops on a broiler rack and cook under preheated a medium-high broiler for 5–6 minutes on each side, or until cooked through. Serve with a mixed vegetable salad.

char siu beef with broccoli

Serves **4**
Preparation time **15 minutes**
Cooking time **10 minutes**

4 cups **baby broccoli**,
  thinly sliced
low-calorie cooking spray
2 **garlic cloves**, finely chopped
1 tablespoon peeled and
  grated **fresh ginger root**
1 lb **ground round** or **ground
  sirloin beef**
¼ cup **Chinese rice wine**
⅓ cup **char siu sauce**
  (Chinese barbecue sauce)
⅓ cup **roasted peanuts,**
  coarsely chopped
1 **red chile,** seeded and thinly
  sliced

Blanch the broccoli in a saucepan of boiling water for
1–2 minutes. Drain and set aside.

Spray a large, nonstick wok or skillet with cooking
spray and heat over high heat. Add the garlic, ginger,
and ground beef and stir-fry, breaking up the beef with a
wooden spoon, for 3–4 minutes, until the meat is browned.

Add the rice wine and char siu sauce and simmer
for 1 minute. Add the broccoli and cook, stirring, for
1–2 minutes, until heated through.

Remove the pan from the heat and sprinkle with the
peanuts and chile. Serve with rice noodles.

For hoisin beef with peas, spray a large, nonstick wok
or skillet with low-calorie cooking spray and heat over
high heat. Add the garlic, ginger, and ground beef and
stir-fry for 3–4 minutes as in the recipe above. Add the
rice wine as above with ⅓ cup hoisin sauce and simmer
for 1–2 minutes. Stir in 1⅓ cups fresh or frozen peas
and cook for 3–4 minutes, until just tender. Stir in a
handful of chopped mint and serve with noodles.

pork with honey & ginger

Serves **4**
Preparation time **15 minutes**,
  plus marinating
Cooking time **10 minutes**

1 lb lean **pork**, thinly sliced
1 teaspoon **cornstarch**
2 teaspoons peeled and finely
  chopped **fresh ginger root**
2 tablespoons **dark soy sauce**
2 tablespoons **honey**
2 tablespoons **Chinese
  rice wine**
2 teaspoons **Chinese
  five-spice powder**
1 teaspoon **sesame oil**
3 tablespoons **peanut oil**
1 **green bell pepper**, cored,
  seeded, and cubed
3 **scallions**, cut into 2 inch
  lengths
1 tablespoon **malt vinegar**
1 tablespoon **light soy sauce**
2 tablespoons **water**
squeeze of **lime juice**
salt and **white pepper**

Put the pork into a bowl and sprinkle with the cornstarch. Add the ginger, dark soy sauce, honey, rice wine, Chinese five-spice powder, and sesame oil and toss to coat evenly. Cover and let marinate at room temperature for 30 minutes, or up to overnight in the refrigerator, then drain the pork.

Heat half the peanut oil in a nonstick wok or large skillet over high heat until the oil starts to shimmer. Add half the pork and stir-fry for 2 minutes, then remove with a slotted spoon. Wipe the pan clean with paper towels. Heat the remaining oil in the pan and stir-fry the rest of the pork in the same way.

Return all the pork to the pan, add the green bell pepper, scallions, vinegar, light soy sauce, and measured water and cook, stirring, for another 3 minutes, until the pork is well browned and the bell pepper has softened slightly.

Season with salt and white pepper to taste, then add the lime juice. Serve with rice and lime wedges, if desired.

For mussels with honey & ginger, follow the recipe above, replacing the pork with 2 lb scrubbed and debearded live mussels (see page 150), discarding any open ones that do not close when tapped, and omitting the cornstarch. Heat 1 tablespoon peanut oil in a wok or large skillet over high heat. Add the ginger as above and stir-fry for a few seconds, then add the dark soy sauce, honey, rice wine, and sesame oil. Bring to a boil, add the mussels, and simmer, covered, for 2–3 minutes, until opened, discarding any that remain closed. Stir in the scallions, light soy sauce, and lime juice and serve.

red braised lamb

Serves **4–6**
Preparation time **15 minutes**
Cooking time **about 3 hours**

1¾ lb boneless lean **lamb
  shoulder,** cut into
  bite-size cubes
thumb-size piece of **fresh
  ginger root,** peeled and cut
  into matchsticks
4 **garlic cloves,** chopped
1 **onion,** sliced
1 teaspoon **Chinese
  five-spice powder**
1 **star anise**
1 **cinnamon stick**
1 teaspoon **black
  peppercorns,** crushed
2 **cardamom pods,** crushed
1 tablespoon **tomato paste**
⅓ cup **Chinese rice wine**
3 tablespoons **dark soy sauce**
2 tablespoons **light soy sauce**
3 tablespoons packed
  dark brown sugar
2 cups **water** or **chicken
  stock**

To garnish
sliced **scallions**
sliced **red chiles**

Put all the ingredients into a heavy, flameproof
casserole dish or Dutch oven with a tight-fitting lid,
pouring over the measured water or stock at the end.
Bring to a simmer on the stove.

Cover the casserole dish and transfer to a preheated
oven, at 300°F, for about 3 hours, until the lamb is
meltingly tender.

Remove the casserole dish from the oven and garnish
the lamb with sliced scallions and red chiles. Serve with
egg noodles or rice.

For Chinese-style lamb burgers, put 1¾ lb lean
ground lamb in a bowl with 2 teaspoons each of grated
garlic and peeled fresh ginger root, 2 finely chopped
scallions, 2 teaspoons Chinese five-spice powder, and
1 tablespoon each of light soy sauce and sweet chili
sauce. Season with salt and black pepper and mix with
your fingers until well combined. Cover and chill in the
refrigerator for 1–2 hours, or overnight if time permits.
Divide the mixture into 8 portions and form each one
into a patty. Cook under a preheated medium-high
broiler for 4–5 minutes on each side, or until cooked
to your preference. Serve with a chopped mixed salad.

hoisin pork, rice & greens

Serves **4**

Preparation time **15 minutes**,
plus marinating

Cooking time **20–25 minutes**

1 cup **quick-cooking long-
grain rice**

3 tablespoons **hoisin sauce**

2 **garlic cloves**, crushed

2 inch piece of **fresh ginger
root**, peeled and grated

1 **red chile**, seeded and sliced

1 **star anise**

1 tablespoon **tomato paste**

10 oz lean **pork tenderloin**,
cut into thin strips

low-calorie cooking spray

1 **red onion**, chopped

1 ⅓ cups finely chopped
cabbage or **collard greens**

1 **carrot**, thinly sliced

salt

toasted sesame seeds,
to serve

Cook the rice in a saucepan of salted boiling water for 16–18 minutes, or according to the package directions, until just tender. Drain and set aside.

Meanwhile, mix together the hoisin sauce, garlic, ginger, chile, star anise, and tomato paste in a bowl. Add the pork and toss to coat evenly. Cover and let marinate in a cool place for up to 1 hour, then drain the pork.

Spray a nonstick wok or large skillet with cooking spray and heat over high heat. Add the pork and stir-fry for about 2 minutes, until browned and cooked through. Stir in the onion, cabbage or collard greens, and carrot, followed by the rice. Toss together for about 3 minutes, until the rice is piping hot. Sprinkle with toasted sesame seeds and serve immediately.

For hoisin lamb with stir-fry noodles, follow the recipe above, omitting the rice, replacing the pork with 10 oz lamb cutlets, and omitting the tomato paste. Marinate and then stir-fry the lamb and the vegetables as above. Add 3 (7 oz) packages precooked stir-fry rice noodles (or 1 lb dried rice noodles, cooked according to the package directions) to the pan and toss together for about 1 minute, until heated through. Sprinkle with chopped cilantro leaves instead of sesame seeds to serve.

braised beef in ginger & garlic

Serves **4**

Preparation time **25 minutes**

Cooking time **2¼ hours**

low-calorie cooking spray

1½ lb lean **boneless beef chuck** or **beef round**, cut into bite-size pieces

2 **onions**, thickly sliced

2 tablespoons peeled and grated **fresh ginger root**

4 **garlic cloves**, crushed

2 teaspoons **Chinese five-spice powder**

4 **star anise**

1 **cinnamon stick**

1 **dried red chile**

10 **black peppercorns**

2 tablespoons packed **light brown sugar**

½ cup **light soy sauce**

¼ cup **tomato paste**

7¼ cups **rich beef stock**

Spray a large, flameproof casserole dish or Dutch oven with a tightly fitting lid with cooking spray and heat over high heat. Add half the beef and stir-fry for 5–6 minutes, until browned. Transfer to a plate with a slotted spoon. Respray the casserole with cooking spray, stir-fry the rest of the beef in the same way, and transfer to the plate.

Wipe the casserole clean with paper towels, spray again lightly with cooking spray, and heat over medium heat. Add the onions, ginger, garlic, and spices and stir-fry for 1 minute, then add the sugar, soy sauce, and tomato paste. Return the beef and any juices to the casserole, then stir in the stock to just about cover and bring to a gentle simmer.

Cover the casserole tightly, transfer to a preheated oven, at 325°F, and cook for 2 hours, or until the beef is meltingly tender.

Serve in warm bowls with steamed rice.

For beef, ginger & garlic stir-fry, spray a nonstick wok or large skillet with low-calorie cooking spray and heat over high heat. Add 6 sliced scallions, 2 tablespoons peeled and grated fresh ginger root, and 4 finely chopped garlic cloves and stir-fry for 30 seconds. Add 1 lb thinly sliced lean sirloin steak and stir-fry for 2–3 minutes, or until just cooked and sealed. Stir in a large handful of bean sprouts, ⅔ cup oyster sauce and ⅔ cup beef stock. Cook, stirring, over high heat for 3–4 minutes, until bubbling. Remove from the heat and serve with steamed rice.

mu shu pork

Serves **4**
Preparation time **15 minutes**
Cooking time **10 minutes**

low-calorie cooking spray
1 ¼ lb lean **ground pork**
2 **garlic cloves**, crushed
2 teaspoons peeled and
   grated **fresh ginger root**
⅓ cup **light soy sauce**
3 tablespoons **oyster sauce**
2 tablespoons **Chinese
   rice wine**
1 **carrot**, cut into matchsticks
1 **red bell pepper**, cored,
   seeded, and thinly sliced
4 oz **shiitake mushrooms**,
   thinly sliced
6 **scallions**, thinly sliced
   diagonally, plus extra to
   garnish
3 cups finely shredded
   napa cabbage
2 teaspoons **sesame oil**

Spray a large, nonstick wok or skillet with cooking spray and heat over high heat. Add the pork and stir-fry, breaking it up with a wooden spoon, for 2–3 minutes, until browned. Transfer to a bowl. Add the soy sauce, oyster sauce, and rice wine to the pork in the bowl.

Wipe the pan clean with paper towels, respray with cooking spray, and heat over high heat. Add the carrot, red bell pepper, and mushrooms and stir-fry for 2–3 minutes, until softened, then add the scallions, cabbage, and pork mixture and stir-fry for 2–3 minutes, until the cabbage has just wilted.

Remove the pan from the heat, stir in the sesame oil, and serve immediately, garnished with sliced scallion.

For mu shu pork fried rice, follow the recipe above, replacing the cabbage with 1 cup jasmine rice or long-grain rice, freshly cooked and cooled. Once added to the pan, stir-fry for 4–5 minutes, until piping hot. Remove the pan from the heat and stir in ¼ cup sweet chili sauce, then toss to mix and serve immediately.

lamb with sugar snap peas

Serves **4**

Preparation time **10 minutes**, plus marinating

Cooking time **10 minutes**

2 teaspoons **cornstarch**

1½ tablespoons **Chinese rice wine**

2 tablespoons **light soy sauce**

2 **garlic cloves**, finely chopped

1 lb boneless lean **lamb cutlets**, cut into thin slices

1 teaspoon **Sichuan peppercorns**

¼ teaspoon **kosher salt**

3 tablespoons **peanut oil**

1 cup trimmed and diagonally sliced **sugar snap peas** (cut into thirds)

1 teaspoon **sesame oil**

1 **red chile,** seeded and finely chopped

1 **scallion**, finely shredded

Mix the cornstarch with the rice wine in a bowl until smooth, then stir in the soy sauce and garlic. Add the lamb and toss to coat evenly. Cover and let marinate at room temperature for 25–30 minutes, then drain the lamb.

Put the Sichuan peppercorns into a dry wok or large skillet and stir over medium heat until they begin to pop and release their aroma. Transfer to a mortar, add the salt, and pound with a pestle until coarsely ground.

Heat half the peanut oil in the pan over high heat until the oil starts to shimmer. Add half the lamb and stir-fry for 3 minutes, then remove with a slotted spoon. Add the remaining peanut oil to the pan and stir-fry the rest of the lamb in the same way.

Return all the lamb to the pan, add the sugar snap peas, and stir-fry for 1 minute. Add the sesame oil, chile, scallion, and the ground salt and pepper mixture, and stir-fry for another minute. Serve immediately with noodles, if desired.

For scallops with snow peas & Sichuan pepper,
follow the recipe above, replacing the lamb with 12 cleaned scallops. After marinating as above, stir-fry in 2 batches as above. Return to the pan and add 1 cup halved snow peas instead of the sugar snap peas with the other ingredients, then continue as above.

beef with yellow bell peppers

Serves **4**

Preparation time **10 minutes**

Cooking time **8 minutes**

½ tablespoon **peanut oil**

1 tablespoon **black bean sauce**

12 oz **sirloin** or **tenderloin steak**, sliced

1 **red chile,** seeded and cut into strips

1 **onion**, cut into large dice

2 large **yellow bell peppers**, cored, seeded, and cut into large dice

1 cup boiling **beef stock**

1 teaspoon **cornstarch**, mixed to a paste with 1 tablespoon **cold water**

Heat the oil in a wok or large skillet over high heat until the oil starts to shimmer. Add the black bean sauce and stir-fry for a few seconds, then add the sliced beef and stir-fry for about 1 minute, until cooked halfway.

Mix in the chile, onion, and bell peppers and stir-fry for 1–2 minutes, then add the hot stock and bring to a boil.

Stir in the cornstarch paste gradually and cook, stirring constantly, until the sauce has thickened and become transparent. Serve immediately with Spicy Tomato Dipping Sauce (see below).

For spicy tomato dipping sauce, to serve as an accompaniment, heat 3½ cup tomato puree or tomato sauce in a wok or large skillet with 2 tablespoons each of Chinese rice wine and water, 1 tablespoon light soy sauce, and 1 teaspoon chili oil. Simmer until reduced to a thick sauce, then set aside to cool before serving.

chinese barbecue pork

Serves **4–6**

Preparation time **10 minutes**,
   plus marinating and resting

Cooking time **20 minutes**

1¾ lb lean **pork tenderloin**

⅓ cup **char siu sauce**
   (Chinese barbecue sauce)

2 tablespoons **honey**

Cut the pork in half lengthwise. Using a sharp knife, cut slits into both sides of the pork in a crisscross pattern. Put the char siu sauce into a shallow glass or ceramic dish, add the pork, and turn to coat evenly. Cover and let marinate in the refrigerator for 1 hour, or overnight if time permits.

Put a roasting rack or wire rack over a roasting pan. Pour cold water into the pan to a depth of 1 inch. Lay the pork on the rack and drizzle with half the honey. Put the pan under a preheated high broiler about 4 inches from the heat source and cook for 10–12 minutes, until browned.

Turn the pork over, drizzle with the remaining honey, and cook for 8–10 minutes, until just cooked through. Remove from the broiler, cover with aluminum foil, and let rest for 12–15 minutes before thinly slicing. Serve with steamed rice and steamed Chinese greens.

For Chinese barbecue lamb cutlets, put 8 boneless lean lamb cutlets, about 4–5 oz each, into a shallow glass or ceramic dish. Mix together 2 tablespoons light soy sauce, 1 tablespoon honey, 2 teaspoons each of crushed garlic and fresh ginger root, and 3 tablespoons char siu sauce (Chinese barbecue sauce). Brush over the lamb to coat evenly, cover, and let marinate in the refrigerator for 1 hour. Place on a broiler rack in a single layer and cook under a preheated medium-high broiler for 3–4 minutes on each side, or until cooked to your liking. Serve with a crisp green salad.

five-spice beef stir-fry

Serves **4**

Preparation time **20 minutes**, plus marinating

Cooking time **10 minutes**

3 lean **top sirloin steaks,** about 7 oz each

1½ cups **sugar snap peas**

1 **carrot**

6 **baby corn**

low-calorie cooking spray

1 **red chile,** thinly sliced

1 small **onion,** sliced

1½ cups **broccoli florets**

1¼ cups hot **vegetable stock**

2 tablespoons **light soy sauce**

1 tablespoon **cornstarch,** mixed to a paste with 2 tablespoons **cold water**

salt and **white pepper**

scallions, to garnish

Marinade

2 teaspoons **Chinese five-spice powder**

2 **garlic cloves,** crushed

2 teaspoons ground **Sichuan peppercorns**

1 tablespoon **dark soy sauce**

½ teaspoon **dried red pepper flakes**

2 tablespoons **Chinese rice wine**

Slice the beef into thin strips and put into a glass or ceramic bowl with all the ingredients for the marinade. Toss to coat evenly, cover and let marinate in the refrigerator for 3–4 hours, or overnight if time permits.

Trim the sugar snap peas, cut the carrots into thin matchsticks, and halve the baby corn lengthwise.

Spray a large, nonstick wok or skillet with cooking spray and heat over high heat. Add the beef mixture and stir-fry for 2–3 minutes, until browned and sealed.

Add the chile and onion to the pan and stir-fry for 1 minute, then add the remaining vegetables and stir-fry for another 1–2 minutes. Add the stock and soy sauce and stir well.

Bring to a boil, add the cornstarch paste, and stir to mix thoroughly. Cook, stirring constantly, for 2–3 minutes, until the mixture has thickened.

Remove the pan from the heat and season to taste with salt and white pepper. Ladle into warm bowls and serve with steamed rice and shredded scallion to garnish.

For ground pork & five-spice noodle stir-fry,

follow the recipe above, replacing the steak with 1¼ lb lean ground pork and breaking it up with a wooden spoon while stir-frying. To serve, cook 1¼ lb fresh egg noodles according to the package directions, divide among 4 warm, wide bowls, and top with the pork and vegetable mixture.

pork with brown rice

Serves **4**

Preparation time **15 minutes**

Cooking time **30 minutes**

1 cup **long-grain brown rice**

1 tablespoon **sunflower oil**

12 oz boneless, lean **pork**, thinly sliced into large slices, halved crosswise

2 **garlic cloves**, finely chopped

3–4 cups **vegetables for stir-frying**, such as strips of bell pepper, bean sprouts, broccoli florets, sliced leeks, and carrot sticks

1½ cups **apple juice**

2 teaspoons **tomato paste**

1 teaspoon **Chinese five-spice powder**

Bring a saucepan of water to a boil, add the brown rice, and simmer for 30 minutes, or until just tender.

Meanwhile, when the rice is nearly cooked, heat the oil in a nonstick wok or large skillet over high heat until the oil starts to shimmer. Add the pork and garlic and stir-fry for 3 minutes. Add the vegetables and stir-fry for 3 minutes.

Mix the apple juice with the tomato paste and Chinese five-spice powder in a small bowl, pour the mixture into the pan, and cook for 1 minute.

Drain the rice, spoon it into warm bowls, and top with the pork stir-fry.

For brown rice with shrimp, onion & bell peppers,

follow the recipe above, replacing the pork with 8 oz raw, peeled jumbo shrimp and stir-frying with the garlic for 1 minute. Add 1 red and 1 green bell pepper, each cored, seeded, and finely chopped, and 1 thinly sliced red onion, then continue with the recipe as above.

spicy beef with scallions

Serves **4**

Preparation time **10 minutes**

Cooking time **15 minutes**

3 tablespoons **oyster sauce**

2 tablespoons **Chinese rice wine**

2 teaspoons **dried red pepper flakes** or 2 **dried red chiles**, halved

½ cup **beef stock**, cooled

1 teaspoon **honey**

1 tablespoon **cornstarch**

low-calorie cooking spray

1 lb lean **top sirloin steak**, thinly sliced

12 **scallions**, diagonally cut into 1½ inch pieces

Mix together the oyster sauce, rice wine, chile, stock, honey, and cornstarch in a small bowl until smooth.

Spray a large, nonstick wok or skillet with cooking spray and heat over high heat until smoking hot. Add the steak and stir-fry for 3–4 minutes, until browned and sealed.

Stir in the oyster sauce mixture, then add the scallions and continue cooking, stirring frequently, for 10 minutes, or until the steak is tender.

For chicken, chile & vegetable stir-fry, follow the recipe above, replacing the beef with 1 lb chicken breast, cut into bite-size rectangular pieces, and adding 1 small finely julienned carrot and 1½ cups snow peas, thinly sliced lengthwise, instead of the scallions.

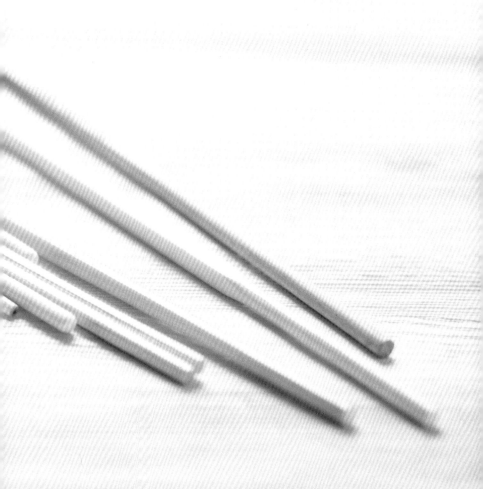

poultry

chinese clay-pot chicken

Serves **4**

Preparation time **15 minutes**

Cooking time **20–25 minutes**

1 tablespoon **cornstarch**

½ teaspoon **sesame oil**

2 tablespoons **dark soy sauce**

⅓ cup **Chinese rice wine**

1¼ lb **skinless chicken thighs**, cut into bite-size pieces

low-calorie cooking spray

3 **garlic cloves**, thinly sliced

1 tablespoon peeled and finely grated **fresh ginger root**

1½ cups trimmed **snow peas**

1 **red bell pepper**, cored, seeded, and cut into bite-size pieces

1 cup **chicken stock**

1 **cinnamon stick**

Mix together the cornstarch, sesame oil, half the soy sauce, and 1 tablespoon of the rice wine in a bowl until smooth. Add the chicken and toss to coat evenly.

Spray a large, nonstick wok or skillet with cooking spray and heat over high heat until smoking. Add the chicken and stir-fry for 4–5 minutes, until lightly browned. Transfer to a plate.

Wipe the pan clean with paper towels, respray with cooking spray, and heat over medium heat. Add the garlic and ginger and stir-fry for 30 seconds, then add the snow peas and red bell pepper and stir-fry for another 3–4 minutes or until tender.

Return the chicken to the pan and stir in the stock, cinnamon stick, and the remaining soy sauce and rice wine. Reduce the heat to medium and simmer, stirring occasionally, for 12–15 minutes, until the chicken is cooked through and the sauce is reduced. Discard the cinnamon, then serve in warm bowls with steamed rice.

For Chinese-style ground chicken & mushroom braise, mix together 1 tablespoon cornstarch,
1 teaspoon each of sesame oil, grated garlic, and fresh ginger root, and 1 tablespoon each of dark soy sauce and Chinese rice wine in a large bowl. Add 1¼ lb ground chicken and combine. Spray a large, nonstick wok with low-calorie cooking spray and heat over high heat. Add the chicken mixture and stir-fry for 4–5 minutes, until browned. Stir in 3 cups thinly sliced cremini mushrooms and 1⅓ cups frozen peas. Stir-fry for 3–4 minutes, then stir in 1 cup chicken stock and 2 tablespoons light soy sauce. Bring to a boil, then reduce the heat and cook for 3–4 minutes, until thickened. Serve with rice.

chicken & sweet chili packages

Serves **4**

Preparation time **15 minutes**

Cooking time **20–25 minutes**

4 **shallots**, thinly sliced

4 **skinless chicken breast**s,
about 5 oz each

¼ cup **dark soy sauce**

2 tablespoons **kecap manis
(Indonesian sweet soy
sauce)**

¼ cup **sweet chili sauce**

¼ cup **Chinese rice wine**

thumb-size piece of **fresh
ginger root**, peeled and cut
into fine shreds

2 **garlic cloves**, finely chopped

4 **star anise**

To garnish

shredded **scallion**

finely diced **red chile**

Cut four 12 inch squares of aluminum foil. Place a sliced shallot and a chicken breast in the center of each foil square. Bring the sides of each square up around the chicken to form "cups."

Mix together the soy sauce, kecap manis, sweet chili sauce, and rice wine in a small bowl, then divide among the packages. Add the ginger, garlic, and star anise to each package and fold the edges together to seal and form packages.

Put the packages onto a baking sheet and bake in a preheated oven, at 350°F, for 20–25 minutes, or until the chicken is cooked through, opening one of the packages and checking that the juices run clear when the thickest part of the meat is pierced with the tip of a sharp knife.

Serve the chicken thickly sliced, garnished with shredded scallion and red chile, with noodles.

For steamed cod & black bean packages, follow the recipe above, replacing the chicken with 4 thick, skinless cod fillets and using ¼ cup black bean sauce instead of the sweet chili sauce. Assemble the packages as above and bake in the oven for 12–15 minutes, or until the fish is cooked through, opening one of the packages and checking that the flesh is opaque in the center and just flaking.

98

hoisin duck pancakes

Serves **4**
Preparation time **20 minutes**
Cooking time **10 minutes**

4 boneless **duck breasts,**
about 7 oz each, skinned
2 teaspoons **ground white**
pepper
2 **garlic cloves,** crushed
1 teaspoon peeled and grated
fresh ginger root
½ teaspoon **Chinese**
five-spice powder
2 teaspoons **sesame oil**
low-calorie cooking spray
½ cup **hoisin sauce,** plus
extra for dipping
2 tablespoons **sweet**
chili sauce
8 **scallions,** shredded
½ **cucumber,** halved, seeded,
and cut into thin matchsticks
12 **Chinese rice pancakes**

Cut the duck breasts into thin strips and put into a bowl.

Mix together the white pepper, garlic, ginger, five-spice powder, and sesame oil in a small bowl.

Spray a large, nonstick wok or skillet with cooking spray and heat over high heat. Add the duck and spices and stir-fry for about 3–4 minutes, until the duck is just cooked through but still slightly pink in the center, then add the hoisin sauce and sweet chili sauce and cook, stirring, for 1–2 minutes, until the duck is well coated with the sauce.

Transfer the duck to a warm dish. Arrange the scallions and cucumber in a serving bowl.

Warm the pancakes according to the package directions, then serve for each person to top with some of the duck, scallions, and cucumber, roll up, and eat straight away with extra hoisin sauce to dip into.

For warm Chinese duck & bok choy salad, follow the recipe above to cook the duck. Spray a nonstick wok with low-calorie cooking spray and heat over high heat. Add 2 teaspoons each of grated fresh ginger root and garlic, 1 finely chopped and seeded red chile, and 4 cups coarsely shredded bok choy, and stir-fry for about 3–4 minutes, until the bok choy has wilted. Stir in the cooked duck, toss to mix well, and serve on warm plates.

chicken & cashew nut stir-fry

Serves **4**
Preparation time **15 minutes**
Cooking time **10 minutes**

1 tablespoon **peanut oil**
1 teaspoon **Sichuan pepporcorns**
4 **cloves**
1 teaspoon **fennel seeds**
1 **star anise**
2 **dried red chiles**
1 **cinnamon stick**
1 **red onion**, sliced
3 large **skinless chicken breasts**, about 6 oz each, thinly sliced
1 tablespoon peeled and finely chopped **fresh ginger root**
1 tablespoon **Chinese rice wine**
1 teaspoon **dark soy sauce**
2 tablespoons **light soy sauce**
1 tablespoon **black rice vinegar**
2 teaspoons packed **light brown sugar**
1 cup **raw unsalted cashew nuts**, lightly toasted
¼ cup **water**
6 **scallions**, thinly sliced

Heat the oil in a large, nonstick wok or skillet over high heat until the oil starts to shimmer. Add the whole spices and cook for a few seconds until fragrant.

Stir in the onion, chicken, and then all the remaining ingredients except the measured water and scallions. Stir-fry for 4–5 minutes, tossing to mix well.

Add the measured water to the pan and stir-fry for another 3–4 minutes, or until the chicken is cooked through, then stir in the scallions. Serve in warm bowls with rice or noodles.

For cashew nut & scallion fried rice, spray a nonstick wok or large skillet with low-calorie cooking spray and heat over high heat. Add 2 teaspoons each of peeled and grated fresh ginger root and garlic, 1 finely chopped red chile, and 6 thinly sliced scallions and stir-fry for 1 minute. Add 1 cup lightly toasted raw unsalted cashew nuts and stir-fry for 1–2 minutes, then add 1 cup jasmine rice or long-grain rice, freshly cooked and cooled, and stir-fry for 3–4 minutes, until it is piping hot. Serve immediately.

sesame chicken drumsticks

Serves **4**

Preparation time **10 minutes**,
plus marinating

Cooking time **45–50 minutes**

12 large **chicken drumsticks**,
skinned

lettuce leaves, to serve

Marinade

2 teaspoons grated **fresh
ginger root**

2 teaspoons grated **garlic**

2 teaspoons **Chinese
five-spice powder**

⅓ cup **soy sauce**

⅓ cup **sweet chili sauce**

3 tablespoons **tomato paste**

finely grated zest and juice of
1 **orange**

1 teaspoon **sesame oil**

Make 3–4 slashes in each chicken drumstick with a
sharp knife and put into a glass or ceramic bowl.

Mix together all the marinade ingredients in a small
bowl and then pour over the chicken. Toss to coat
evenly, cover, and let marinate in the refrigerator for
6–8 hours, or overnight if time permits, turning the
chicken occasionally.

Transfer the chicken and marinade to a nonstick
roasting pan and arrange the chicken in an even
layer. Roast in a preheated oven, at 400°F, turning
occasionally and basting with the marinade and juices,
for 45–50 minutes, or until sticky and golden and
cooked through; the juices should run clear when
the thickest part of the meat is pierced with the tip
of a sharp knife.

Serve the chicken warm or at room temperature
on a bed of lettuce leaves with steamed rice.

For stir-fry sesame beef, slice 4 lean sirloin steaks,
about 7 oz each, thinly and put into a bowl with the
marinade ingredients as above. Cover and let marinate
in the refrigerator for 1–2 hours, or longer if time
permits. Spray a large, nonstick wok or skillet with low-
calorie cooking spray and heat over high heat. Add the
beef and marinade and stir-fry for about 4–5 minutes,
until just cooked through. Serve with rice or noodles.

stir-fried duck breast salad

Serves **4**

Preparation time **15 minutes**, plus cooling

Cooking time **5 minutes**

3 tablespoons **peanut oil**

1 lb boneless, **skinless duck breasts**, cut into thin slices

1 **carrot**

4 inch piece of **cucumber**

¼ head **iceberg lettuce**, finely shredded

1 **celery stick**, thinly sliced diagonally

4 **scallions**, thinly sliced diagonally

handful of **mint leaves**, torn

salt and **black pepper**

Dressing

3 tablespoons **light olive oil**

2 tablespoons **malt vinegar**

2 tablespoons **light soy sauce**

2 teaspoons packed **light brown sugar**

Heat half the oil in a nonstick wok or large skillet over high heat until the oil starts to shimmer. Toss in half the duck, season with salt and black pepper, and stir-fry for about 2 minutes, until browned but still slightly pink in the center. Remove with a slotted spoon and wipe the pan clean with paper towels. Heat the remaining oil in the pan and stir-fry the rest of the duck in the same way.

Toss the cooked duck in a large bowl with all the ingredients for the dressing. Let stand at room temperature while you prepare the rest of the salad.

Use a vegetable peeler to slice the carrot thinly lengthwise into paper-thin ribbons. Cut the cucumber in half lengthwise and scoop out the seeds, using a spoon. Place, cut side down, on a cutting board and thinly slice diagonally.

Put the carrot and cucumber into a large bowl, then add the lettuce, celery, scallions, and mint.

Let the duck cool completely in the dressing, then toss it with the prepared salad.

For crunchy scallop salad, heat 2 tablespoons peanut oil in a wok or large skillet, add 12 cleaned scallops, and stir-fry for about 4 minutes, until golden and just cooked. Toss in a large bowl with the dressing ingredients as above, then let stand while you prepare the rest of the salad following the recipe above. Once the scallops are completely cooled, toss with the prepared salad.

chicken & chestnut braise

Serves **4**
Preparation time **10 minutes**
Cooking time **50 minutes**

8 large bone-in **chicken
  thighs**, skinned
2 tablespoons peeled and
  grated **fresh ginger root**
6 **scallions**, coarsely sliced
24 **cooked, peeled chestnuts**
¼ cup **Chinese rice wine**
2½ cups **chicken stock**
1½ tablespoons packed **dark
  brown sugar**
2 tablespoons **dark soy sauce**
salt and **black pepper**

Put all the ingredients into a heavy, flameproof casserole dish or Dutch oven and bring to a boil.

Cover the dish, reduce the heat to low (use a heat diffuser if possible), and simmer gently for about 45 minutes, until the chicken is cooked through and tender, stirring occasionally.

Season with salt and black pepper, then serve with steamed rice and steamed Chinese greens.

For spicy lamb & mushroom stew, follow the recipe above, replacing the chicken with 1 ¼ lb boneless lean lamb cutlets, cut into bite-size pieces, adding 3 dried red chiles and using 12 oz thickly sliced shiitake mushrooms instead of the chestnuts. After bringing to a boil, simmer gently, covered, for about 45 minutes, or until the lamb is tender. Serve with rice or noodles.

orange roasted chicken thighs

Serves **4**

Preparation time **5 minutes**,
  plus marinating

Cooking time **30–35 minutes**

12 bone-in **chicken thighs**,
  skinned

Marinade

finely grated zest and juice of
  1 orange

2 tablespoons packed **dark
  brown sugar**

2 teaspoons **Chinese
  five-spice powder**

2 tablespoons **dark soy sauce**

1 tablespoon **light soy sauce**

1 tablespoon **toasted
  sesame oil**

Place the chicken in a single layer in a glass or ceramic dish. Mix together all the ingredients for the marinade in a small bowl and then pour it over the chicken. Toss to coat evenly, cover, and let marinate in the refrigerator for at least 30 minutes, or overnight if time permits.

Transfer the chicken and marinade to a nonstick roasting pan and arrange the chicken in an even layer. Roast in a preheated oven, at 375°F, turning the chicken twice, for 30–35 minutes, or until golden and cooked through; the juices should run clear when the thickest part of the meat is pierced with the tip of a sharp knife.

Serve the chicken hot or cold with steamed rice and steamed vegetables.

For quick orange seared scallops, put 25 large, cleaned scallops into a glass or ceramic bowl. Mix together the ingredients for the marinade as above, pour it over the scallops, and toss to coat evenly. Spray a large, nonstick wok or skillet with low-calorie cooking spray and heat over high heat. Add the scallops and marinade and stir-fry for 2–3 minutes, being careful not to overcook them. Serve with cooked noodles.

kung pao chicken

Serves **4**

Preparation time **25 minutes**, plus marinating

Cooking time **20 minutes**

3 large skinless **chicken breasts**, about 6 oz each

¼ cup **white wine vinegar**

⅓ cup **light soy sauce**

2 tablespoons **cornstarch**

6 **dried red chiles**, broken into pieces and seeded

2 teaspoons **Sichuan peppercorns**, lightly crushed

3 tablespoons packed **light brown sugar**

3 tablespoons **tomato paste**

1¼ cups **chicken stock**

low-calorie cooking spray

8 **scallions**, diagonally sliced

3 **garlic cloves** finely chopped

1 **red bell pepper**, seeded and cut into ½ inch pieces

3 cups canned **sliced bamboo shoots**, drained

3 cups canned **water chestnuts**, coarsely chopped

4 cups **baby spinach leaves**

salt and **black pepper**

Cut the chicken into 1 inch cubes and put into a wide glass or ceramic bowl.

Mix together 2 tablespoons of the vinegar, 3 tablespoons of the soy sauce, 1 tablespoon of the cornstarch, the chiles, Sichuan peppercorns, and half the sugar in a small bowl. Pour the marinade over the chicken and toss to coat evenly. Cover and let marinate in the refrigerator for about 30 minutes.

Combine the remaining vinegar and soy sauce, tomato paste, and stock with the remaining cornstarch and sugar.

Spray a heavy nonstick skillet with cooking spray and heat over high heat until just smoking. Add the chicken and marinade and stir-fry for 5–6 minutes, or until browned and just cooked through. Add the scallions, garlic, red bell pepper, bamboo shoots, and water chestnuts and stir-fry for 3–4 minutes.

Add the stock mixture and bring to a boil, stirring constantly. Reduce the heat and cook gently, stirring, for about 5–6 minutes, until the sauce has thickened. Check the seasoning and adjust, if necessary.

Line a shallow serving dish with the baby spinach leaves. Spoon the chicken mixture on top and serve immediately.

For Sichuan pork with snow peas & carrots, follow the recipe above, replacing the chicken with 1¼ lb lean pork tenderloin, cut into small bite-size pieces, and using 1½ cups trimmed snow peas and 1 small carrot, cut into matchsticks, instead of the red bell pepper. Cook as above, then serve over steamed rice in place of the spinach leaves.

low-fat lemon chicken

Serves **4**

Preparation time **15 minutes**, plus marinating

Cooking time **8 minutes**

1 **egg**, lightly beaten

2 **garlic cloves**, sliced

2 small pieces of **lemon zest**, plus the juice of **1 lemon**

1 lb **skinless chicken breasts**, cut into ¼ inch slices

2 tablespoons **cornstarch**

1 tablespoon **canola oil** or **olive oil**

1 **scallion**, diagonally sliced into ¾ inch lengths

lemon slices, to garnish

Mix together the egg, garlic, and lemon zest in a shallow glass or ceramic dish. Add the chicken and toss to coat evenly, then cover and let marinate at room temperature for 10–15 minutes.

Remove the lemon zest and add the cornstarch to the marinated chicken. Mix well to distribute the cornstarch evenly among the chicken slices.

Heat the oil in a nonstick wok or large skillet over high heat until the oil starts to shimmer. Add the chicken slices, making sure you leave a little space between them, and cook for 2 minutes on each side.

Reduce the heat to medium and stir-fry for another minute, or until the chicken is browned and cooked through. Increase the heat and pour in the lemon juice. Add the scallion, garnish with lemon slices, and serve immediately with steamed rice.

For warm lemon chicken & herb salad, cook the chicken as above, then toss in a bowl with ½ sliced cucumber,, a handful of cilantro leaves, 6 torn basil leaves, and 2 cups arugula. Dress the salad lightly with ½ teaspoon sesame oil and 1 teaspoon canola oil or olive oil.

chicken & snow pea stir-fry

Serves **4**
Preparation time **20 minutes**
Cooking time **15 minutes**

1 ¼ lb **skinless chicken
thighs**, skinned and cut
into thin strips
3 **garlic cloves**, crushed
2 teaspoons **Chinese
five-spice powder**
1 teaspoon **dried red
pepper flakes**
¼ cup **light soy sauce**
low-calorie cooking spray
1 **onion**, cut into wedges
5 cups trimmed **snow peas**
2 tablespoons **dark soy sauce**

To garnish
small handful of **cilantro
leaves**, chopped
chile slivers
thinly sliced **cucumber ribbons**

Combine the chicken, garlic, five-spice powder, red pepper flakes, and 2 tablespoons of the light soy sauce in a bowl.

Spray a large, nonstick wok or skillet with cooking spray and heat over high heat until just smoking. Add the onion and snow peas and stir-fry for about 3–4 minutes, until lightly charred and tender. Transfer to a bowl.

Wipe the pan clean with paper towels, respray with cooking spray, and heat over high heat. Add the chicken mixture and stir-fry for 4–5 minutes, or until browned and just cooked through. Return the onion and snow peas to the pan and add the remaining light soy sauce and the dark soy sauce. Cook, stirring, for about 2–3 minutes, until heated through.

Ladel into warm bowls, garnish with the cilantro leaves, chile sliver,s and cucumber ribbons and serve with rice or noodles.

For shrimp and snow pea stir-fry, follow the recipe above, replacing the chicken with 1 ¼ lb raw peeled jumbo shrimp. Cook the shrimp mixture as for the chicken mixture above until they have turn pinked and are firm, then continue with the recipe.

spiced duck & cabbage stir-fry

Serves **4**

Preparation time **25 minutes**, plus marinating

Cooking time **20 minutes**

3 large boneless **duck breasts**, about 7 oz each, skinned

¼ cup **dark soy sauce**

2 teaspoons **Chinese five-spice powder**

1 teaspoon **Sichuan peppercorns**, crushed

2 **garlic cloves**, crushed

2 teaspoons peeled and finely grated **fresh ginger root**

low-calorie cooking spray

chopped **cilantro**, to garnish

Cabbage

thumb-size piece of **fresh ginger root**, peeled and cut into thin matchsticks

2 **red chiles**, seeded and thinly sliced

1 head of **napa cabbage**, shredded

1 large **carrot**, cut into thin matchsticks

3 tablespoons **light soy sauce**

2 **shallots**, halved and thinly sliced

Slice the duck thinly and put into a wide glass or ceramic bowl with the soy sauce, five-spice powder, crushed Sichuan peppercorns, garlic, and ginger. Toss to mix well, cover, and let marinate at room temperature for 20–30 minutes.

Spray a large, nonstick wok or skillet with cooking spray and heat over high heat. Add the duck mixture and stir-fry for 5–6 minutes, until browned but still pink in the center. Transfer to a bowl, cover, and keep warm.

Wipe the pan clean with paper towels, respray with cooking spray, and heat over medium-high heat. Add the ginger and chiles and stir-fry for 2–3 minutes. Add the cabbage and carrot and stir-fry for 3–4 minutes, or until the cabbage has softened. Stir in the soy sauce and shallots and continue to stir-fry for 1–2 minutes.

Transfer the stir-fried cabbage to warm serving plates and divide the duck strips on top of each portion. Garnish with chopped cilantro and serve.

For Chinese five-spice broiled duck breasts, skin 4 duck breasts, about 7 oz each, score in a crisscross pattern all over with a sharp knife and put into a wide glass or ceramic dish. Mix together ¼ cup dark soy sauce, 2 tablespoons honey, 2 teaspoons Chinese five-spice powder, and 1 teaspoon each of grated fresh ginger root and garlic in a bowl. Spoon over the duck and toss to coat evenly, then cover and let marinate in the refrigerator for at least 1 hour. When ready to cook, place the duck in a single layer under a preheated medium broiler and cook for 4–5 minutes on each side, or until cooked to your preference. Thickly slice and serve immediately with steamed bok choy and rice.

chinese chicken with bell peppers

Serves **4**

Preparation time **10 minutes**,
  plus marinating

Cooking time **20 minutes**

2 inch piece of **fresh ginger
  root**, peeled and grated
2 **garlic cloves**, chopped
2 **star anise**
1/3 cup **teriyaki marinade**
3 boneless **chicken breasts**,
  about 6 oz each, diced
low-calorie cooking spray
1/2 **red bell pepper**, cored,
  seeded, and diced
1/2 **green bell pepper**, cored,
  seeded, and diced
1/2 **yellow bell pepper**, cored,
  seeded, and diced
2 **scallions**, sliced
1 1/2 cups **quick-cooking
  long-grain rice**
2 1/2 cups **chicken stock**
salt and **black pepper**

Mix together the ginger, garlic, star anise, and teriyaki marinade in a glass or ceramic bowl. Add the chicken and toss to coat evenly, then cover and let marinate at room temperature for 10 minutes.

Meanwhile, spray a large, nonstick wok or skillet with cooking spray and heat over medium heat. Add the bell peppers and stir-fry for 3 minutes.

Add the scallions, rice, and chicken to the pan, then pour in the stock. Season to taste with salt and black pepper and simmer for 15 minutes, until the rice is just tender. Serve immediately.

For pork with green bell peppers & litchis, follow the recipe above, replacing the chicken with 1 lb diced lean pork. Instead of the mixed bell peppers, stir-fry 1 1/2 cored, seeded, and diced green bell peppers and stir 2 cups drained, canned litchis into the pan with the scallions, rice, and pork.

chicken with black bean sauce

Serves **4**
Preparation time **15 minutes**
Cooking time **15 minutes**

low-calorie cooking spray
1 **red onion**, thinly sliced
2 **red bell peppers**, cored,
   seeded, and thinly sliced
2 **garlic cloves**, crushed
2 **red chiles**, seeded and
   finely chopped
4 skinless **chicken breasts**,
   about 5–6 oz each,
   thinly sliced
6 **scallions**, diagonally sliced
   into 1 ½ inch pieces
2 teaspoons **cornstarch**
⅓ cup **black bean sauce**
2 tablespoons **Chinese
   rice wine**
½ cup **chicken stock**
   or **beef stock**, cooled

Spray a large, nonstick wok or skillet with cooking spray and heat over high heat. Add the red onion and red bell peppers and stir-fry for 1–2 minutes.

Add the garlic, chiles, and chicken to the pan and stir-fry over high heat for about 5–6 minutes, or until the chicken is sealed and tender. Add the scallions and stir-fry for another minute.

Mix the cornstarch with the black bean sauce, rice wine, and stock in a small bowl until smooth. Stir into the pan and cook, stirring constantly, for 2–3 minutes, until the mixture has thickened slightly. Serve with boiled or steamed rice.

For shrimp with scallions & black bean sauce,
follow the recipe above, replacing the chicken with 1 ¼ lb raw, peeled jumbo shrimp. When the dish is cooked, remove the pan from the heat and stir in a small handful of finely chopped cilantro leaves.

sweet & sour chicken

Serves **4**
Preparation time **20 minutes**
Cooking time **20 minutes**

1 ¼ cups **pineapple juice**
2 **garlic cloves**, crushed
2 teaspoons peeled and
    grated **fresh ginger root**
2 tablespoons **dark soy sauce**
2 tablespoons **white wine**
    vinegar
2 tablespoons **honey**
¼ cup **ketchup**
¼ teaspoon **dried red**
    pepper flakes
low-calorie cooking spray
1 **onion**, thickly sliced
1 **red bell pepper**, seeded
    and cut into small bite-size
    pieces
1 **yellow bell pepper**, seeded
    and cut into small bite-size
    pieces
4 skinless **chicken breasts**,
    about 6 oz each, cut into
    bite-size pieces
1 ¼ cups **pineapple chunks**
2 tablespoons **cornstarch**,
    mixed to a paste with
    ¼ cup **cold water**

Put the pineapple juice into a small bowl and stir in the garlic, ginger, soy sauce, vinegar, honey, ketchup, and red pepper flakes until thoroughly combined. Set aside.

Spray a large, nonstick wok or skillet with cooking spray and heat over high heat. Add the onion and bell peppers and stir-fry for about 3–4 minutes, until just tender. Add the chicken and stir-fry for 4–5 minutes, until lightly browned.

Add the pineapple juice mixture and pineapple chunks to the pan and bring to a simmer over medium heat. Cook, stirring frequently, for 4–5 minutes, until the chicken is cooked through.

Stir in the cornstarch paste and cook, stirring constantly, for 3–4 minutes, until the sauce has thickened. Serve with noodles or Light Egg Fried Rice (see page 224).

For classic sweet & sour pork, follow the above recipe, replacing the chicken with 1 ¼ lb pork tenderloin, cut into bite-size pieces. When the dish is ready, serve with egg noodles.

sticky ginger chicken stir-fry

Serves **4**
Preparation time **10 minutes**
Cooking time **10 minutes**

1 lb **skinless chicken
  breasts**, quartered
  lengthwise
thumb-size piece of **fresh
  ginger root**, peeled and cut
  into matchsticks
3 tablespoons **sweet
  chili sauce**
low-calorie cooking spray
3 cups **snow peas**
16 **baby zucchini**, thinly
  sliced lengthwise
2 cups thickly sliced
  napa cabbage
8 **scallions**, thinly sliced
small handful of **cilantro
  leaves**

Mix together the chicken, ginger, and 1 tablespoon of
the sweet chili sauce in a bowl.

Spray a large, nonstick wok or skillet with cooking
spray and heat over high heat. Add the chicken and
stir-fry for about 4–5 minutes, until lightly browned.

Add the snow peas, zucchini, and cabbage to the pan
and stir-fry for 4–5 minutes, or until the chicken is
cooked through and the vegetables are just tender.

Stir in the scallions and remaining sweet chili sauce
and cook for another few seconds until heated through.
Sprinkle with the cilantro leaves and serve with steamed
rice or noodles.

For quick shrimp & vegetable stir-fry, follow
the recipe above, replacing the chicken with 1 ¼ lb
raw, peeled, and deveined jumbo shrimp and using
1 (12 oz) package stir-fry vegetables of your choice
instead of the snow peas, zucchini, and cabbage.

roasted chicken & plum sauce

Serves **4**

Preparation time **10 minutes**,
  plus resting

Cooking time **1½ hours**

1 **chicken**, about 3 lb

2 tablespoons **Chinese
  five-spice powder**

1 tablespoon **Sichuan
  peppercorns**, crushed

1 tablespoon **peanut oil**

8 **plums**, halved and
  pits removed

1 cup **Chinese rice wine**

⅔ cup **vegetable stock**

2 tablespoons **honey**,
  or to taste

salt and **black pepper**

Put the chicken into a roasting pan and pat the skin dry
with paper towels. Mix together the five-spice powder,
crushed Sichuan peppercorns, and oil in a small bowl.
Rub over the chicken as evenly as possible and season
with salt and black pepper. Roast in a preheated oven,
at 400°F, for 30 minutes.

Place half the plums around the chicken and pour the
rice wine and stock over them. Return to the oven and
roast for another 30 minutes.

Add the remaining plums to the roasting pan and roast
for 20–25 minutes, or until the chicken is cooked through
(cover the chicken with aluminum foil if it is browning too
fast); the juices should run clear when the thickest part of
the thigh is pierced with the tip of a sharp knife.

Transfer the chicken to a warm srving plate and let rest
in a warm place. Heat the plum mixture in the roasting
pan on the stove over high heat. Stir in the honey to
taste and season well with salt and black pepper. Serve
the chicken with the plum sauce, steamed Chinese
greens, and rice or egg noodles.

For broiled duck with plum sauce, skin 4 duck
breasts, about 7 oz each, score in a crisscross pattern all
over with a sharp knife, and place in a single layer on a
nonstick baking sheet. Mix together ⅓ cup plum sauce,
2 tablespoons light soy sauce, and 1 teaspoon Chinese
five-spice powder in a bowl. Spoon the marinade over
the duck to coat evenly, cover, and let marinate in the
refrigerator for 1–2 hours, or overnight. Cook under a
preheated medium-high broiler for 4–5 minutes on each
side, or until cooked to your preference.

fish & seafood

sesame swordfish packages

Serves **4**
Preparation time **20 minutes**
Cooking time **20 minutes**

4 **swordfish** or **shark fillets**,
   about 7 oz each,
   pin boned and skinned
3 oz **shiitake mushrooms**,
   sliced
1 cup halved **sugar snap
   peas** (cut lengthwise)
1 **mild red chile,** seeded
   and thinly sliced
2 tablespoons **sesame oil,**
   plus extra for brushing
1 inch piece **fresh ginger
   root**, peeled and grated
2 **garlic cloves,** crushed
2 tablespoons **light soy sauce**
2 tablespoons **lime juice**
2 tablespoons **sweet
   chili sauce**
¼ cup chopped **cilantro**

Cut four 12 inch squares of nonstick parchment paper and brush the centers with sesame oil. Place a fish fillet in the center of each square. Mix together the mushrooms, sugar snap peas, and chile, then divide among the paper, piling on top of the fish. Bring the sides of each square up around the fish to form "cups."

Mix together the sesame oil, ginger, and garlic and spoon over the vegetables. Fold the edges of the paper to seal and form packages and place on a baking sheet.

Bake in a preheated oven, at 375°F, for 20 minutes, or until the fish is cooked through (open a package and check the flesh is opaque in the center).

Meanwhile, mix together the soy sauce, lime juice, sweet chili sauce, and cilantro. Loosen the packages and spoon the dressing over the fish before serving.

For Asian mussel packages, divide 2 lb scrubbed and debearded fresh mussels, discarding any open ones that do not close when tapped, 1 finely chopped red chile, 1 inch piece of finely chopped fresh ginger root, and 1 chopped garlic clove among 4 large squares of nonstick parchment paper. Bring the sides of each square up around the mussels. Mix together ½ cup coconut milk and 1 tablespoon Thai fish sauce, season, and divide among the paper squares, then fold over the edges of the paper to seal the packages. Place on a baking sheet and bake in a preheated oven, at 400°F, for 6–8 minutes, until all the mussels have opened, opening up one of the packages to check. Discard any that remain closed. Sprinkle with a little chopped cilantro and serve with bread.

ginger & garlic shrimp

Serves **4**
Preparation time **20 minutes,**
    plus marinating
Cooking time **15 minutes**

1¼ lb **raw jumbo shrimp,**
    peeled with tails left intact
low-calorie cooking spray
1 large **onion,** thickly sliced
3 cups thin **broccoli florets**
1 large **carrot,** halved and
    thinly sliced diagonally
8 **scallions,** diagonally sliced
    into 1¼ inch lengths
1 inch piece of **fresh ginger
    root,** peeled and finely
    shredded
½ cup **chicken stock**
1 tablespoon **oyster sauce**

Marinade
⅓ cup **light soy sauce**
4 **garlic cloves,** crushed
2 teaspoons **Sichuan
    peppercorns,** crushed
2 tablespoons **rice vinegar**
1 tablespoon **cornstarch**

Put the shrimp into a glass or ceramic bowl and add
all the ingredients for the marinade. Toss to coat
evenly, cover, and let marinate at room temperature
for 10 minutes.

Meanwhile, spray a large, nonstick wok or skillet with
cooking spray and heat over high heat. Add the onion
and stir-fry for about 3–4 minutes, until softened. Add
the broccoli, carrot, scallions, and ginger and stir-fry for
about 3–4 minutes, until just tender. Stir in the stock
and cook for 2–3 minutes.

Stir the shrimp mixture and oyster sauce into the pan
and cook, stirring, for 3–4 minutes, until the shrimp have
turned pink and are firm. Serve with rice or noodles.

For Chinese-style shrimp salad, put 1 lb cooked,
peeled shrimp into a wide salad bowl with the leaves
from 2 small butterhead lettuce and 3 cups halved
cherry tomatoes. Mix together 1 finely chopped red
chile, 2 tablespoons each light olive oil and sweet chili
sauce, the juice of 1 lemon, and 1 teaspoon each honey
and Chinese five-spice powder in a small bowl. Season
to taste with salt and black pepper, pour the dressing
over the salad, and toss to mix well before serving.

chili scallops with gai lan

Serves **4**

Preparation time **10 minutes**

Cooking time **10 minutes**

6 cups 2½ inch **gai lan**
(Chinese broccoli) pieces

20 **scallops**, shelled and
cleaned

2 tablespoons **Chinese
chili jam** (available from
Chinese grocers)

low-calorie cooking spray

2 **garlic cloves**, finely chopped

2 teaspoons peeled and finely
chopped **fresh ginger root**

1 **onion**, thinly sliced

2 teaspoons **light soy sauce**

Put the gai lan into a bamboo steamer, then cover and
steam over a wok or large saucepan of boiling water
(see page 14) for 2–3 minutes, until just tender. Drain
and keep warm.

Meanwhile, toss the scallops with 1 tablespoon of the
chili jam in a bowl. Spray a large, nonstick skillet with
cooking spray and heat over medium-high heat. Add the
scallops and stir-fry for 1 minute on each side, until just
cooked. Remove from the pan and cover to keep warm.

Wipe the pan clean with paper towels, respray with
cooking spray, and heat over medium heat. Add the
garlic, ginger, and onion and stir-fry for 3–4 minutes,
until softened. Add the remaining chili jam and the gai
lan, tossing to coat. Remove from heat and stir in the
scallops and soy sauce. Ladle into warm bowls and
serve with steamed rice or noodles.

For steamed chili scallops, shell and clean 16 scallops,
reserving the shells. Place a teaspoon of Chinese chili
jam in the bottom of each shell, followed by the scallop.
Slice 4 scallions thinly and divide among the scallops.
Drizzle ¼ teaspoon light soy sauce over each scallop.
Place in stacking bamboo steamer baskets, cover, and
steam over a wok or large saucepan of boiling water
(see page 14) for 5–8 minutes, depending on their
size, until firm to the touch. If you don't have stacking
baskets, steam in 2–3 batches; cover and keep the
cooked batches warm while cooking the remainder.
To serve, arrange the scallop shells on plates and serve
with steamed rice and stir-fried Chinese greens.

orange-soy salmon with noodles

Serves **4**
Preparation time **5 minutes**
Cooking time **13 minutes**

low-calorie cooking spray
4 **skinless salmon fillets**,
   about 6 oz each, any stray
   bones removed
8 oz **dried soba noodles**
2 teaspoons **sesame oil**
2 tablespoons **sesame seeds**
¼ cup **dark soy sauce**
2 tablespoons **orange juice**
2 tablespoons **mirin** (Japanese
   sheet rice wine) or **sherry**

Spray a heavy skillet with cooking spray and heat over high heat. Add the salmon and cook for 3–4 minutes on each side, until browned. Remove, wrap loosely in aluminum foil, and let rest for 5 minutes.

Cook the noodles in a large saucepan of boiling water for about 5 minutes, or according to the package directions, until just tender. Drain well and toss with the sesame oil and seeds.

Meanwhile, combine the soy sauce, orange juice, and mirin or sherry in a small bowl. Pour the sauce into the skillet and bring to a boil, then reduce the heat and simmer for 1 minute.

Divide the noodles among 4 warm bowls and serve with the salmon and sauce and steamed sugar snap peas on the side.

For salmon, orange & soy packages, cut four 12 inch squares of aluminum foil. Place a salmon fillet in the center of each foil square. Bring the sides of each square up around the salmon to form "cups" and add the soy sauce, orange juice, and mirin or sherry as above, along with 2 sliced scallions, 2 sliced garlic cloves, and 2 teaspoons peeled and grated fresh ginger root. Fold the edges of the foil together to seal and form packages, place on a baking sheet, and bake in a preheated oven, at 400°F, for about 15 minutes, or until the fish is cooked through, opening one of the packages and checking that the flesh is opaque in the center and just flaking. Remove and let rest briefly, then serve with steamed rice.

chinese tea-marinated trout

Serves **4**

Preparation time **10 minutes**,
plus infusing, cooling and
marinating

Cooking time **15 minutes**

2 **Lapsang Souchong tea
bags** steeped in 1 cup
boiling hot water

1 tablespoon peeled and
grated **fresh ginger root**

1 **garlic clove**, crushed

¼ cup **kecap manis
(Indonesian sweet
soy sauce)**

2 tablespoons **sweet chili
sauce**

1 tablespoon **honey**

4 **trout fillets**, about 4 oz each

1 tablespoon **sesame oil**

2 tablespoons **peanut oil**

8 oz **baby bok choy**,
halved lengthwise

Once the tea bags have steeped for 5 minutes, discard the bags. Stir in the ginger, garlic, kecap manis, sweet chili sauce, and honey until well blended. Let cool.

Lay the trout fillets in a shallow glass or ceramic dish and pour the tea mixture over them. Cover and let marinate in the refrigerator for at least 4 hours, or overnight if time permits, turning the fish occasionally.

Remove the fish, reserving the marinade, and pat dry on paper towels. Heat the sesame oil with 1 tablespoon of the peanut oil in a large, nonstick skillet, add the fish, skin side down, and cook for 2–3 minutes. Turn the fish over and cook for 3 minutes. Transfer to a warm plate and cover with aluminum foil; it will continue cooking in its own steam while you cook the bok choy.

Heat the remaining oil in the pan over high heat, add the bok choy and stir-fry until just beginning to wilt. Pour in half the reserved marinade, bring to a boil, and cook for 3–4 minutes, until most of the liquid has evaporated and the bok choy is tender. Serve with the trout.

For trout & shrimp fish cakes, put 12 oz trout fillets, skinned and coarsely chopped, 8 oz chopped, raw peeled jumbo shrimp, 1 teaspoon each finely grated garlic and fresh ginger root, 1 seeded and finely chopped red chile, a small handful of chopped cilantro, 1 beaten egg, 1 teaspoon dark soy sauce, and 1 cup dried bread crumbs in a food processor. Season with salt and black pepper and process until mixed. Shape into 12 round cakes. Arrange on a baking sheet lined with lightly greased nonstick parchment paper and bake in a preheated oven, at 400°F, for 15–20 minutes, until lightly browned and cooked through.

squid & vegetable stir-fry

Serves **4**
Preparation time **15 minutes**
Cooking time **10 minutes**

1 tablespoon **peanut oil**

2 teaspoons **sesame oil**

2 **leeks**, trimmed, cleaned,
and thinly sliced

2 **celery sticks**, thinly sliced

1 **carrot**, cut into thin
matchsticks

1 **red bell pepper**, seeded
and thinly sliced

1 ½ cups coarsely chopped
bok choy

12 oz cleaned **squid**, cut
into thick rings

2 teaspoons **Chinese
five-spice powder**

¼ cup **light soy sauce**

2 tablespoons **Chinese
rice wine**

3 tablespoons **sweet
chili sauce**

salt and **black pepper**

Heat the oils in a large, nonstick wok or skillet over high heat. Add the leeks, celery, carrot, and red bell pepper and stir-fry for about 3–4 minutes, until softened.

Add the bok choy, squid, and five-spice powder to the pan and stir-fry for 2–3 minutes, until the squid is just cooked through, being careful not to overcook otherwise it will turn rubbery.

Stir in the soy sauce, rice wine, and sweet chili sauce, season with salt and black pepper, and heat through, stirring. Serve with cooked rice or noodles.

For grilled five-spice squid, put 1 ½ lb cleaned squid on a clean work surface, make a cut down one side of each body tube, and open out. Using a sharp knife, lightly score the inside of the flesh in a crisscross pattern to help tenderize it, then cut into bite-size pieces, along with the tentacles. Mix together the juice of 1 lime, 1 tablespoon light olive oil, 1 finely chopped red chile, and 2 teaspoons each of grated garlic and peeled fresh ginger root and Chinese five-spice powder in a small bowl. Rub into the squid in a shallow glass or ceramic dish, cover, and let marinate at room temperature for 10–15 minutes. Heat a nonstick, ridged grill pan until smoking hot. Remove the squid from the marinade, add to the pan, in batches, and cook on each side for no more than 2 minutes, pushing the squid down with the back of a spatula. Serve hot.

sichuan sea bass

Serves **4**
Preparation time **20 minutes**
Cooking time **25 minutes**

low-calorie cooking spray
4 thick sea bass fillets, about
   7 oz each, skinned
6 **scallions**, diagonally sliced
   into 1 ¼ inch lengths
2 **red bell peppers**, cored,
   seeded, and thinly sliced
4 **bok choy**, thickly sliced
⅓ cup **water**
¼ cup **light soy sauce**
salt

Sauce
3 **garlic cloves**, finely chopped
2 tablespoons peeled and finely
   chopped **fresh ginger root**
2 **red chiles**, finely chopped
6 **scallions**, finely chopped
2 teaspoons **Sichuan**
   peppercorns, crushed
2 tablespoons **tomato paste**
1 tablespoon **hot chili sauce**
1 tablespoon **light soy sauce**
3 tablespoons **rice vinegar**
½ cup **chicken stock**

Spray a wok or skillet with cooking spray and heat
over medium heat. For the sauce, add the garlic, ginger,
chiles, and scallions and stir-fry for about 2–3 minutes,
until softened. Stir in the crushed peppercorns, tomato
paste, and hot chili sauce and cook, stirring, for a few
seconds. Add the soy sauce, vinegar, and stock to the
pan, bring to a simmer, and cook for 2–3 minutes, until
thickened slightly.

Make 3–4 deep, diagonal slashes in the skin of the fish
with a sharp knife. Arrange the fish on a baking sheet
lined with parchment paper, season with salt, and brush
with the sauce. Put into a preheated oven, at 400°F, for
15–20 minutes, until the fish is cooked through.

Meanwhile, spray a separate nonstick wok or skillet
with cooking spray and heat over medium heat. Add the
scallions and stir-fry for 1–2 minutes, until softened. Add
the red bell peppers, bok choy, and measured water and
stir-fry for 3–4 minutes, until the vegetables are just
tender, then stir in the soy sauce. Spoon the vegetables
into the center of 4 warm plates. Top each with a fish
fillet, then spoon some of the sauce over them. Serve
with Quick Stir-fry Rice (see below).

For quick stir-fry rice, to serve as an accompaniment,
spray a large, nonstick wok or skillet with low-calorie
cooking spray and heat over medium-high heat. Add
1 tablespoon mild curry powder, 3 cups frozen peas,
and 1 cup jasmine rice or long-grain rice, freshly cooked
and cooled. Season with salt and black pepper and
stir-fry for 3–4 minutes, or until piping hot. Remove
from the heat, stir in ⅓ cup chopped cilantro, and serve.

chinese steamed oysters

Serves **4**
Preparation time **15 minutes**
Cooking time **10 minutes**

16 large **fresh oysters,**
  unshucked
2 **red chiles**, seeded and
  finely diced
1 tablespoon peeled and finely
  grated **fresh ginger root**
2 teaspoons finely
  grated **garlic**
1 tablespoon **Chinese**
  rice wine
1 tablespoon **light soy sauce**
1 tablespoon **dark soy sauce**
1 teaspoon **chili bean sauce**
1 **scallion**, finely shredded,
  to garnish

Divide the oysters between 2 heatproof plates that
will fit inside 2 large stacking bamboo steamer baskets.
Cover and steam over a wok or large saucepan of
boiling water (see page 14) for 6–7 minutes, or until
the oysters have opened.

Meanwhile, for the sauce, combine all the remaining
ingredients in a small bowl.

Lift the oysters from the steamer baskets and carefully
remove the top shell of each oyster. Spoon a little of the
sauce over each steamed oyster and serve immediately
with shredded scallion and steamed rice, if desired.

For oyster & corn soup, spray a nonstick saucepan
with low-calorie cooking spray and heat over medium
heat. Add 4 thinly sliced scallions and 1 teaspoon
peeled and grated fresh ginger root and stir-fry
for 3–4 minutes, until the scallion is softened but
not browned. Add 20 freshly shucked oysters,
1 (14¾ oz) can creamed corn, 4 cups chicken stock,
and 1 tablespoon Chinese rice wine and bring to a
boil. Reduce the heat and simmer for 5 minutes. Mix
1 tablespoon cornstarch to a paste with 3 tablespoons
cold water. Add to the pan and return to a boil, stirring
constantly. Drizzle 1 lightly beaten egg into the pan and
cook for 2–3 minutes, until the egg has set in strands.
To serve, ladle the soup into warm bowls and garnish
with chopped cilantro.

scallops with lemon & ginger

Serves **3–4**
Preparation time **10 minutes**
Cooking time **10 minutes**

2 tablespoons **vegetable oil**
8 **scallops**, shelled and
   cleaned, then cut into
   thick slices
½ bunch of **scallions**, thinly
   sliced diagonally
½ teaspoon **ground turmeric**
3 tablespoons **lemon juice**
2 tablespoons **Chinese
   rice wine**
2 pieces of **preserved ginger
   with syrup**, chopped
salt and **black pepper**

Heat a wok or large skillet until hot. Add 1 tablespoon of
the oil and heat over medium heat. Add the scallops and
stir-fry for 3 minutes, then remove with a slotted spoon
to a plate.

Add the remaining oil to the pan and heat over medium
heat until the oil starts to shimmer. Add the scallions
and turmeric and stir-fry for a few seconds. Add the
lemon juice and rice wine and bring to a boil, then stir
in the preserved ginger.

Return the scallops and their juices to the pan and toss
until heated through. Season with salt and black pepper
to taste and serve immediately with Fennel & Carrot
Salad (see below).

For fennel & carrot salad, to serve as an
accompaniment, use a vegetable peeler to cut 1 trimmed
fennel bulb and 2 carrots into thin shavings. Toss in a
bowl with a handful of cilantro leaves, the juice of
½ lemon, and ½ teaspoon sesame oil.

mussels with black beans

Serves **4**
Preparation time **25 minutes**
Cooking time **10 minutes**

2 lb **fresh mussels**
1 tablespoon **peanut oil**
4 **garlic cloves**, finely chopped
1 tablespoon peeled and finely
  grated **fresh ginger root**
2 **red chiles**, seeded and
  thinly sliced
2 tablespoons **fermented
  salted black beans**, rinsed
2 tablespoons **Chinese
  rice wine**
2 cups **chicken stock**
  or **fish stock**
6 **scallions**, thickly sliced
3 tablespoons **light soy sauce**
small handful of finely chopped
  cilantro leaves

Clean the mussels thoroughly in cold water, scraping off any barnacles, scrubbing the shells, and pulling off any stringy beards. Discard any open mussels that do not close when tapped.

Heat a large, nonstick wok or skillet over high heat and add the oil. Add the garlic, ginger, chiles, black beans, and rice wine and stir fry for 30 seconds.

Add the mussels, stock, and scallions to the pan and cook, stirring, for 6–8 minutes, until all the mussels have opened, discarding any that remain closed.

Season the mussels with the light soy sauce. Sprinkle with the cilantro and serve immediately, ladled into wide warm bowls.

For mussels & black bean noodle stir-fry, spray a large, nonstick wok or skillet with low-calorie cooking spray and place over high heat. Add 6 sliced scallions, 1 teaspoon each of peeled and grated fresh ginger root and garlic, 12 oz cooked mussels, and 1/3 cup black bean sauce and cook, stirring, for 2–3 minutes. Add 12 oz fresh egg noodles and continue to cook, tossing frequently, for 3–4 minutes, until the noodles are piping hot. Serve immediately in warm bowls.

spiced shrimp with cashew nuts

Serves **4**
Preparation time **15 minutes**
Cooking time **10–15 minutes**

1 lb **raw jumbo shrimp**,
  peeled and butterflied

1 teaspoon **Chinese rice wine**

1 tablespoon **egg white**

1 tablespoon **cornstarch**

1 tablespoon **peanut oil**

6 **dried red chiles**, halved
  and seeded

1 teaspoon **Sichuan**
  peppercorns, crushed

thumb-size piece of **fresh**
  ginger root, finely shredded

3 **garlic cloves**, thinly sliced

4 **scallions**, thickly sliced

½ cup **chicken stock**

1 cup **roasted cashew nuts**

Sauce

1 tablespoon **sugar**

1 tablespoon **cornstarch**

2 tablespoons **dark soy sauce**

2 tablespoons **Chinese**
  rice wine

½ cup **water**

Mix together the shrimp, rice wine, egg white, and cornstarch in a bowl until well combined.

Stir together all the ingredients for the sauce in a small bowl until smooth and set aside.

Heat the oil in a large, nonstick wok or skillet over high heat until almost smoking. Add the shrimp and stir-fry for 3–5 minutes, until just turning pink, then remove with a slotted spoon to a plate.

Add the chiles and crushed Sichuan peppercorns to the pan and stir-fry over high heat for 1–2 minutes, until fragrant. Add the ginger, garlic, and scallions and stir-fry for 30–40 seconds.

Return the shrimp with their juices to the pan and toss to mix. Add the stock and bring to a boil. Stir in the sauce mixture and cook, stirring constantly, until it has thickened. Finally, add the cashew nuts, stir to mix well, and serve immediately.

For spiced shrimp, mango & lemon grass rice,

heat 1 teaspoon peanut oil in a heavy saucepan, add 1 cinnamon stick and 2 each of chopped shallots, red chiles, and garlic cloves, and stir-fry for 2–3 minutes, until the shallots are softened. Add 1 tablespoon hot chili sauce, 2 cups jasmine rice or long-grain rice, and 1 tablespoon lemon grass paste and stir to mix well. Pour in 2½ cups vegetable stock and bring to a boil. Stir in 1 lb raw, peeled jumbo shrimp and the diced flesh of 1 mango. Cover tightly, reduce the heat to low, and cook for 15–20 minutes. Remove from the heat and let stand, covered, for a few minutes before fluffing up with a fork and serving.

steamed ginger fish

Serves **4**
Preparation time **10 minutes**
Cooking time **6–8 minutes**

4 thick **halibut** or **cod fillets**,
 about 7 oz each
thumb–size piece of **fresh
 ginger root**, peeled and
 finely shredded
1 **red chile,** seeded and
 finely shredded
1 tablespoon finely grated
 orange zest
1 tablespoon finely grated
 lemon zest
2 **scallions**, finely shredded
2 tablespoons **light soy sauce**
1 tablespoon finely chopped
 cilantro leaves
salt and **white pepper**

Pat the fish dry with paper towels and season well salt
and white pepper. Place on a heatproof plate that will fit
inside a bamboo steamer and sprinkle evenly with the
ginger, chile, and orange and lemon zests.

Place the plate in the bamboo steamer, cover, and
steam over a wok or large saucepan of boiling water
(see page 14) for 6–8 minutes, until the fish is just
cooked through; the flesh should be opaque in the
center and slightly flaking but still moist.

Remove the plate from the steamer and drain off
any liquid that may have accumulated around the fish.
Sprinkle the scallions over the fish, then drizzle with the
soy sauce and sprinkle with the chopped cilantro. Serve
with Stir-Fry Vegetable Rice (see below) or steamed
rice and steamed Chinese greens.

For stir-fry vegetable rice, to serve as an
accompaniment, spray a large, nonstick wok or skillet
with low-calorie cooking spray and put over high heat
until almost smoking. Add 1 cup jasmine rice or long-
grain rice, freshly cooked and cooled, and stir-fry for
 3 minutes. Add 1 (12 oz) package mixed stir-fry
vegetables and stir-fry for 5 minutes. Season well
with salt and black pepper, then stir in 2 tablespoons
light soy sauce and 4 thinly sliced scallions and cook,
stirring, for 2 minutes. Serve immediately.

salmon with chinese greens

Serves **4**

Preparation time **15 minutes**

Cooking time **25 minutes**

vegetable oil, for oiling

2 cups boiling hot water

4 chunky **salmon steaks**,
about 7 oz each

1 tablespoon **tamarind paste**
blended with ¾ cup
cold water

2–3 tablespoons **light soy
sauce**

½ inch piece of **fresh ginger
root**, peeled and grated

2 teaspoons **sugar**

2 **garlic cloves**, crushed

1 **mild green chile,** thinly sliced

1 teaspoon **cornstarch**, mixed
to a paste with 1 tablespoon
cold water

1 small **bok choy**

8 **scallions**, halved lengthwise

⅓ cup chopped **cilantro
leaves**

Oil a roasting rack or wire rack and put over a roasting pan. Pour the measured hot water into the pan. Lay the salmon steaks on the rack, cover tightly with aluminum foil and cook in a preheated oven, at 350°F, for 15 minutes, or until the salmon is almost cooked through.

Meanwhile, put the tamarind paste and water into a small saucepan. Stir in the soy sauce, ginger, sugar, garlic and chile, and heat through gently for 5 minutes.

Add the cornstarch paste to the tamarind mixture and heat gently, stirring constantly, for 1–2 minutes, until thickened.

Quarter the bok choy lengthwise into wedges and arrange the pieces around the salmon on the rack with the scallions. Replace the foil and return to the oven for another 8–10 minutes, or until the vegetables have wilted.

Stir the cilantro into the sauce. Transfer the fish and greens to warm plates, pour over the sauce, and serve.

For salmon with chile & ginger bok choy, follow the recipe above to cook the salmon. Meanwhile, heat 2 tablespoons sesame oil in a wok or large skillet over high heat, add 1 seeded and finely chopped red chile, ½ inch piece of fresh ginger root, peeled and finely chopped, and the leaves of 3 small heads of bok choy and stir-fry for 1 minute, or until the leaves have wilted. Stir in 2 tablespoons light soy sauce and serve with the cooked salmon.

sweet & sour shrimp

Serves **4**
Preparation time **20 minutes**
Cooking time **10 minutes**

8 **scallions**
3 tablespoons **sweet chili sauce**
3 tablespoons **ketchup**
1 tablespoon packed **light brown sugar**
¼ cup **light soy sauce**
1 tablespoon **Chinese rice wine**
3 tablespoons **water**
low-calorie cooking spray
thumb-size piece of **fresh ginger root**, peeled and cut into fine matchsticks
1¼ lb **raw jumbo shrimp**, peeled and deveined
2 **garlic cloves**, crushed
2 **red chiles**, seeded and finely chopped
10–12 **cherry tomatoes**, halved
1 tablespoon **cornstarch**, mixed to a paste with 2 tablespoons **cold water**

Cut the green tops from the scallions and slice them lengthwise into thin shreds. Set aside for a garnish. Thinly slice the white parts of the scallions diagonally.

Mix together the chili sauce, ketchup, sugar, soy sauce, rice wine, and measured water in a small bowl.

Spray a large, nonstick wok or skillet with cooking spray and heat over high heat. Add the ginger and stir-fry for 30 seconds, then add the shrimp and stir-fry for 2–3 minutes or until the shrimp have turned pink. Remove the shrimp and ginger from the pan to a plate.

Wipe the pan clean with paper towels, respray with cooking spray, and heat over high heat. Add the garlic and chiles, and as soon as they start to sizzle, add the white scallion and cherry tomatoes and stir-fry for 30 seconds. Add the chili sauce mixture and cornstarch paste to the pan and simmer, stirring constantly, for a few seconds until thickened. Return the shrimp with their juices and ginger to the pan with the shredded green scallion and toss to mix well. Serve in warm bowls with egg-fried rice.

For Chinese-style pan-fried shrimp, spray a large skillet with low-calorie cooking spray and heat over high heat. Add 25 raw jumbo shrimp, peeled and deveined, and stir-fry for 3–4 minutes, until they have turned pink. Remove to a warm serving plate. Season and sprinkle with 1 finely chopped red chile and a large handful of chopped cilantro. Mix together ¼ cup sweet chili sauce, 2 tablespoons light soy sauce, and 2 teaspoons sesame oil in a small bowl. Drizzle the dressing over the shrimp, toss to mix, and serve.

seafood congee

Serves **4**

Preparation time **15 minutes**, plus soaking

Cooking time **15 minutes**

4 **dried shiitake mushrooms**

1¼ cups **boiling hot water**

1 tablespoon **peanut oil**

1 teaspoon peeled and grated **fresh ginger root**

2 **shallots**, finely chopped

8 **fresh mussels**, scrubbed and debearded

8 oz cleaned **squid**, cut into rings

8 **raw jumbo shrimp**, peeled and deveined

½ cup **jasmine rice** or **long-grain rice**, freshly cooked and cooled

3¼ cups **vegetable stock** or **chicken stock**

1 tablespoon **Chinese rice wine**

2 tablespoons **light soy sauce**

1 head of **bok choy,** coarsely chopped

small handful of chopped **cilantro** (leaves and stalks)

salt and **white pepper**

Put the dried mushrooms into a small heatproof bowl, pour over the measured water to cover, and let soak for 30 minutes, until softened. Drain and reserve the soaking liquid. Remove and discard the stems, and dice the caps.

Heat a nonstick wok or skillet over high heat, add the oil, and heat until almost smoking. Add the ginger, shallots, and diced mushrooms and stir-fry for a few seconds.

Add all the seafood and stir-fry for 2–3 minutes, until the shrimp are just beginning to turn pink. Add the cooked rice, reserved mushroom soaking liquid, and stock and bring to a boil.

Stir in the rice wine and soy sauce and season to taste with salt and white pepper. Add the bok choy and cilantro and gently simmer for 6–8 minutes, until the seafood is cooked through and all the mussels have opened, discarding any that remain closed. Serve immediately, ladled into warm bowls.

For spicy seafood omelet, to serve 2, beat 4 eggs in a bowl with 1 tablespoon light soy sauce, 1 teaspoon hot chili sauce, and a small handful of chopped cilantro. Heat 1 tablespoon peanut oil in a nonstick skillet over high heat, pour in the egg mixture, and swirl to coat the bottom of the pan evenly. Cook for 6–8 minutes or until almost cooked through and just set. Sprinkle with 6 finely chopped scallions and 8 oz cooked mixed seafood, fold over the sides of the omelet to enclose the filling, then flip over and serve warm with a crisp green salad.

cantonese steamed fish

Serves **4**
Preparation time **15 minutes**
Cooking time **15–18 minutes**

2 whole **sea bass**, about
 1½ oz each, cleaned
 and scaled
2 teaspoons **sea salt**
thumb-size piece of **fresh
 ginger root**, peeled and
 finely shredded
4 **scallions**, finely shredded
1 **red chile,** seeded and finely
 chopped
3 tablespoons **dark soy sauce**
3 tablespoons **light soy sauce**
2 teaspoons **sesame oil**
1 tablespoon **peanut oil**

Make 3–4 deep diagonal slashes in the sides of the fish with a sharp knife. Rub the salt into the slashes and inside the cavity. Put the fish onto a heatproof plate that will fit inside a steamer and sprinkle the ginger over them.

Place the plate in the steamer, cover, and steam for 12–15 minutes, until the fish is just cooked through; the flesh should be opaque in the center and slightly flaking but still moist. Remove the plate from the steamer and drain off any liquid from around the fish. Transfer to a warm, shallow serving plate. Sprinkle the scallions and chile over the fish, then drizzle with the dark and light soy sauces.

Heat the oils together in a small saucepan until smoking, then drizzle over the fish. Serve with boiled rice.

For scallion & ginger fish cakes, put 12 oz coarsely chopped raw peeled shrimp, 10 oz coarsely chopped skinless cod fillet, 6 finely chopped scallions, 1 seeded chopped red chile, 2 teaspoons grated fresh ginger root, 1 teaspoon grated garlic, 1 tablespoon light soy sauce, and a small handful of finely chopped cilantro in a food processor and process until fairly smooth. Transfer to a bowl, cover, and chill in the refrigerator for 6–8 hours. Using slightly wet hands, divide the mixture into 20 portions and shape each into a round cake. Lightly spray a broiler rack with low-calorie cooking spray and arrange the fish cakes on the rack in a single layer. Lightly spray the fish cakes with cooking spray and cook under a preheated medium broiler for 10 minutes, turning halfway, until cooked through and golden brown. Serve with Sweet Chili Dipping Sauce (see page 26).

fish in chili bean sauce

Serves **4**

Preparation time **20 minutes**

Cooking time **10–15 minutes**

1 ¼ lb **cod** or **halibut fillets**, skinned

3 tablespoons **cornstarch**

low-calorie cooking spray

6 **scallions**, thickly sliced diagonally

2 teaspoons finely grated **garlic**

1 tablespoon peeled and finely grated **fresh ginger root**

salt and **white pepper**

Sauce

1 cup **chicken stock**

2 teaspoons **yellow bean sauce**

1 tablespoon **chili bean sauce**

2 tablespoons **Chinese rice wine**

2 teaspoons **dark soy sauce**

2 teaspoons **sesame oil**

Season the fish fillets evenly on both sides with salt. Cut the fish into bite-size pieces and lightly dust with the cornstarch to coat evenly.

Spray a nonstick wok or large skillet with cooking spray and heat over medium heat. Add the fish and cook for 1–2 minutes on each side, until lightly browned. Remove from the pan to a plate.

Wipe the pan clean with paper towels, respray with cooking spray, and heat over high heat. Add the scallions, garlic, and ginger and stir-fry for 30 seconds.

Stir all the sauce ingredients into the pan and season to taste with salt and white pepper. Bring the mixture to a boil, then reduce the heat to a simmer and return the fish to the pan. Simmer for 4–5 minutes, until the fish is cooked through, then serve immediately with steamed rice.

For chili bean salmon salad, arrange 1 (8 oz) package of mixed salad greens on a large plate. Break 1 lb poached skinless salmon fillets into large chunks and arrange over the greens. Mix together the juice of 2 limes, 1 finely chopped red chile, ⅓ cup olive oil, 1 tablespoon chili bean sauce, and 1 teaspoon each honey and light soy sauce in a small bowl. Season with salt and black pepper and drizzle the dressing over the salad. Toss to mix well before serving.

vegetables

spicy sichuan eggplants

Serves **4**

Preparation time **20 minutes**

Cooking time **20 minutes**

2 large **eggplants**, cut into
3/4 x 1½ inch batons

low-calorie cooking spray

1 small **onion**, thinly sliced

4 **garlic cloves**, crushed

2 teaspoons peeled and
grated **fresh ginger root**

1 **red chile,** thinly sliced

3 tablespoons **tomato paste**

1 teaspoon **dried red
pepper flakes**

1 teaspoon **Sichuan
peppercorns**, crushed

½ **red bell pepper**, seeded
and cut into thin strips

½ **yellow bell pepper**, seeded
and cut into thin strips

1 cup **hot vegetable stock**

3 tablespoons **light soy sauce**

1 tablespoon **rice vinegar**

1 teaspoon **honey**

1 tablespoon **cornstarch**,
mixed to a paste with
2 tablespoons **cold water**

6 **scallions**, thinly sliced

chopped **mint** and **cilantro
leaves**, to garnish

Spray the eggplant batons lightly with cooking spray in a large shallow dish and toss to mix well.

Heat a large, nonstick skillet over medium heat, add the eggplants, and stir-fry for 3–4 minutes, until lightly browned. Remove and set aside.

Wipe the pan clean with paper towels, respray with cooking spray, and heat over medium heat. Add the onion, garlic, ginger, and chile and stir-fry for a few seconds. Stir in the tomato paste, red pepper flakes, and crushed peppercorns, then return the eggplants to the pan and add the bell peppers. Pour in the hot stock and bring to a boil, then reduce the heat to medium and simmer for 5–6 minutes, until the eggplant is soft and tender. Add the soy sauce, vinegar, and honey, then stir in the cornstarch paste and cook, stirring constantly, for 3–4 minutes, until the sauce has thickened.

Spoon the eggplant mixture into a large serving dish and sprinkle with the scallions, then garnish with the herbs and serve immediately with rice or noodles.

For quick steamed Chinese eggplants, peel and cut 2 large eggplants into finger-thick batons. Put into 2 stacking bamboo steamer baskets, cover, and steam over a wok or saucepan of boiling water (see page 14) for 10–12 minutes, until tender. Transfer to a warm plate. Make a sauce by mixing together 1 tablespoon each of dark soy sauce, rice vinegar, chili oil, and honey, 1 teaspoon crushed Sichuan peppercorns, 2 tablespoons finely chopped garlic, and 1 tablespoon finely chopped scallion. Pour the sauce over the eggplants and lightly toss to mix. Garnish with cilantro and serve immediately.

broccoli with garlic & ginger

Serves **4**
Preparation time **10 minutes**
Cooking time **5 minutes**

1 small head of **broccoli**,
    divided into florets
2 tablespoons **peanut oil**
2 **garlic cloves**, thinly sliced
2 teaspoons peeled and
    grated **fresh ginger root**
1–2 teaspoons **dried red
    pepper flakes**
salt and **pepper**

Cut the broccoli florets lengthwise into thin slices.

Bring a large saucepan of lightly salted water to a boil. Add the broccoli and blanch for 1–2 minutes. Drain and set aside.

Heat the oil in a large, nonstick wok or skillet over high heat. Swirl the oil around, add the garlic, ginger, and red pepper flakes, and sizzle for 20–30 seconds, until fragrant.

Add the broccoli to the pan and stir-fry for 1–2 minutes, until just tender. Season with salt and black pepper and serve immediately with cooked rice or noodles.

For cauliflower with garlic & sesame, follow the recipe above, replacing the broccoli with 1 small head cauliflower, divided into florets. When the dish is ready, sprinkle with 2 tablespoons toasted sesame seeds and serve immediately.

asparagus & snow pea stir-fry

Serves **4**
Preparation time **10 minutes**
Cooking time **10 minutes**

2 tablespoons **vegetable oil**
1¼ inch piece of **fresh**
  ginger root, peeled
  and thinly shredded
2 large **garlic cloves**,
  thinly sliced
4 **scallions**, diagonally sliced
8 oz thin **asparagus spears**,
  cut into 1¼ inch lengths
2 cups diagonally halved
  snow peas
1½ cups **bean sprouts**
3 tablespoons **light soy sauce**

Heat a large, nonstick wok or skillet over high heat until smoking, then add the oil. Add the ginger and garlic and stir-fry for 30 seconds, then add the scallions and stir-fry for another 30 seconds. Add the asparagus and stir-fry for 3–4 minutes.

Stir the snow peas into the pan and continue stir-frying for 2–3 minutes, until all the vegetables are slightly softened but still crunchy.

Add the bean sprouts and toss for 1–2 minutes, until beginning to wilt, then pour in the soy sauce and toss again. Serve immediately with steamed rice and extra soy sauce, if desired.

For stir-fried vegetable omelets, follow the recipe above to cook the vegetables, then keep warm. For each omelet, beat 3 eggs in a bowl with 2 tablespoons cold water and salt and black pepper. Heat a drizzle of peanut oil in a nonstick skillet over high heat, pour in the egg mixture, and swirl to coat the bottom of the pan evenly. Cook until almost cooked through and just set. Top with one quarter of the cooked vegetables and fold in half, then remove from the pan and keep warm while you make another 3 omelets in the same way, using the remaining cooked vegetables.

noodle pancakes with asparagus

Serves **4**
Preparation time **35 minutes**
Cooking time **30 minutes**

low-calorie cooking spray
2 **garlic cloves**, crushed
1 **red chile**, seeded and finely
  chopped
1 teaspoon peeled and finely
  grated **fresh ginger root**
8 oz **asparagus spears**, tough
  ends discarded and cut into
  2 inch lengths
1 **carrot**, cut into matchsticks
3 cups diagonally halved
  snow peas
1 cup **vegetable stock**
1 tablespoon **cornstarch**
¼ cup **dark soy sauce**
2 tablespoons **sweet
  chili sauce**
2 cup **baby spinach leaves**
10 oz **chow mein noodles**
  (dried Chinese wheat and
  egg noodles), cooked
  according to package
  directions, rinsed with
  cold water, and drained
1 teaspoon **sesame oil**
salt and **black pepper**

Spray a large, nonstick wok with cooking spray and heat. Add the garlic, chile, and ginger and stir-fry for 1 minute. Add the asparagus, carrot, snow peas, and half the stock and bring to a boil, then gently simmer for 2–3 minutes.

Mix the cornstarch and remaining stock in a bowl until smooth. Add to the pan with the soy sauce and chili sauce and simmer, stirring, for 2 minutes, until thickened. Add the spinach and stir until wilted. Remove from the heat.

Spray a separate large, nonstick skillet with cooking spray and heat over high heat. Divide the cooked noodles into 4, add 2 to the pan, and flatten. Reduce the heat to medium and cook for 6–7 minutes, until they develop a crust on the underside. Turn over and cook for 3–4 minutes, flattening as before. Remove from the pan and keep warm while you cook the remaining 2 pancakes.

Season the vegetable mixture with salt and add the sesame oil. Seve each pancake with the vegetables on top.

For asparagus & shrimp noodle stir-fry, prepare 8 oz dried rice noodles according to package directions, until tender. Drain. Spray a nonstick wok with low-calorie cooking spray and heat until smoking. Add 1 lb raw, peeled jumbo shrimp and stir-fry for 3–4 minutes, until they turn pink. Transfer to a plate. Add 1 seeded and thinly sliced red bell pepper, 1 thinly sliced onion, 8 oz asparagus tips, and 1 tablespoon grated fresh ginger root to the pan and stir-fry for 2 minutes, until the onion softens. Whisk 2 tablespoons each of hoisin sauce, sweet chili sauce, and rice vinegar and 1 tablespoon honey in a small bowl. Add with the noodles and shrimp to the pan and toss together for 1–2 minutes, until heated through.

bitter melon with black beans

Serves **4**

Preparation time **25 minutes**

Cooking time **20 minutes**

1¾ lb **bitter melons**

1 tablespoon **peanut oil**

4 **garlic cloves**, finely diced

2 tablespoons peeled and
finely diced **fresh ginger root**

2 **shallots**, finely diced

6 **scallions**, thinly sliced

2 **red chiles**, seeded and
thinly sliced

¼ cup **fermented black
beans**, rinsed and coarsely
chopped

2 teaspoons **sugar**

2 tablespoons **Chinese
rice wine**

1 cup boiling **vegetable stock**

Cut the bitter melons in half lengthwise, remove the seeds with a teaspoon, and discard. Thinly slice the melons.

Bring a large saucepan of water to a boil, add the melons, and blanch for 2–3 minutes. Remove with a slotted spoon and drain well on paper towels.

Heat the oil a large, nonstick wok or skillet over high heat. Add the garlic, ginger, shallots, scallions, chiles, and black beans and stir-fry for 1–2 minutes. Stir in the melon, sugar, rice wine, and stock and bring to a boil, then reduce the heat to medium.

Cover the pan and simmer for 8–10 minutes, until the melon is tender. Serve with steamed rice.

For broccoli with black bean sauce, spray a nonstick wok or large skillet with low-calorie cooking spray and heat over high heat. Add 3 finely chopped garlic cloves, 6 cups thinly sliced broccoli florets, 1 thinly sliced onion, and 8 oz thinly sliced shiitake mushrooms and stir-fry for 3–4 minutes, until the vegetables are slightly softened. Add ¼ cup black bean sauce, 2 tablespoons light soy sauce, and ½ cup vegetable stock and cook, stirring, for 2–3 minutes. Sprinkle with 1 tablespoon toasted sesame seeds and serve with noodles.

sichuan potato stir-fry

Serves **4**

Preparation time **30 minutes**,
  plus standing

Cooking time **15 minutes**

4 red skinned or **white
  round potatoes**

1 tablespoon **peanut oil**

6 **garlic cloves**, coarsely
  chopped

1 tablespoon peeled and finely
  chopped **fresh ginger root**

2 tablespoons finely chopped
  pickled ginger

2 teaspoons **dried red
  pepper flakes**

1 tablespoon **sugar**

2 tablespoons **Chinese
  rice wine**

2 teaspoons **chili oil**

2 teaspoons ground **Sichuan
  peppercorns**

salt and **white pepper**

Peel the potatoes, then cut into thin matchsticks and put into a large bowl with 2 teaspoons salt. Cover with cold water and let stand for 8–10 minutes. Drain thoroughly and pat dry with paper towels.

Heat the oil a large, nonstick wok or skillet over high heat. Add the garlic, fresh ginger, pickled ginger, and red pepper flakes and stir fry for about 30 seconds. Season with salt and white pepper, then add the potatoes and gently stir-fry for a minute or so until well coated with the spices and flavorings.

Add the sugar and rice wine and continue to stir-fry gently for 8–10 minutes, until most of the water has evaporated and the potatoes are tender. Add the chili oil, sprinkle with the Sichuan pepper, and serve immediately.

For Chinese-style potato salad, put 4 peeled, diced, and cooked red-skinned or white round potatoes into a wide salad bowl with 6 thinly sliced scallions, 1 seeded and thinly sliced red chile, a small handful of finely chopped cilantro leaves, and 1 seeded and finely diced red bell pepper. In a separate bowl, mix together ½ cup light mayonnaise, 1 tablespoon each of honey, light soy sauce, and sesame oil, and 1 teaspoon Chinese five-spice powder. Stir to mix well, season with salt and black pepper to taste, and pour the dressing over the potatoes. Toss to mix well and serve.

mixed vegetable stir-fry

Serves **4**
Preparation time **10 minutes**
Cooking time **15 minutes**

low-calorie cooking spray
1 **onion**, sliced
2 **garlic cloves**, crushed
1 **red bell pepper**, cored,
    seeded, and thinly sliced
1 **yellow bell pepper**, cored,
    seeded, and thinly sliced
1 ½ cups **broccoli florets**
12 **baby corn**, halved
8 **baby zucchini**, diagonally
    sliced into ¾ inch lengths
1 cup rinsed and drained,
    canned **sliced bamboo
    shoots**
¾ cup rinsed and drained,
    canned **sliced water
    chestnuts**
3 tablespoons **light soy sauce**
1 tablespoon **cornstarch**
⅓ cup **vegetable stock**
thumb-size piece of **fresh
    ginger root**, grated and juice
    squeezed out and reserved
2 tablespoons **sweet chili
    sauce**
½ cup canned **bean sprouts**,
    rinsed and drained

Spray a large, nonstick wok or skillet with cooking spray and heat over medium heat. Add the onion and garlic and stir-fry for 3 minutes, then add the bell peppers and stir-fry for another 3 minutes.

Add the broccoli florets, baby corn, and zucchini to the pan and continue to stir-fry for 5 minutes. Add the bamboo shoots and water chestnuts and toss to mix in.

Mix together the soy sauce, cornstarch, stock, ginger juice, and sweet chili sauce in a small bowl until smooth.

Make a space in the center of the stir-fried vegetables with a wooden spoon so that the bottom of the pan is visible. Pour in the sauce mixture, bring to a boil, and cook, stirring constantly, until it starts to thicken. Toss the vegetables to coat thoroughly with the sauce.

Transfer to a warm serving dish, sprinkle with the bean sprouts, and serve immediately.

For quick bamboo shoot & water chestnut soup,
bring 5 cups vegetable stock to a boil in a saucepan. Add 4 sliced shiitake mushrooms, 1 (8 oz) can sliced bamboo shoots, rinsed and drained, and 1 (8 oz) can sliced water chestnuts, rinsed and drained, 1 chopped tomato, and 6 sliced scallions. Return to a boil. Mix 1 tablespoon cornstarch to a paste with 2 tablespoons cold water and add to the soup with 2 tablespoons light soy sauce and 1 tablespoon sesame oil. Cook, stirring, for 2–3 minutes, until thickened, then ladle into warm bowls and serve.

chinese greens in garlic sauce

Serves **4**
Preparation time **10 minutes**
Cooking time **10 minutes**

low-calorie cooking spray
6 **garlic cloves**, crushed
1 cup **vegetable stock**
1 tablespoon **dark soy sauce**
1 teaspoon **honey**
2 heads of **bok choy**, thickly
    sliced lengthwise
1 lb **choy sum**, thickly sliced
8 **scallions**, cut into
    1½ inch lengths
1 tablespoon **cornstarch,**
    mixed to a paste with
    3 tablespoons **cold water**
small handful of chopped
    cilantro leaves
1 tablespoon peeled and finely
    julienned **fresh ginger root**
1 teaspoon ground **white**
    pepper

Spray a large, nonstick wok or skillet with cooking spray and heat over medium heat. Add the garlic and stir-fry for 1–2 minutes, until lightly browned.

Pour the stock, soy sauce, and honey into the pan, mix well, and bring to a simmer. Add the bok choy, choy sum, and scallions and cook, stirring, for 2–3 minutes, until softened.

Stir the cornstarch paste into the pan, mixing well, then add the cilantro, ginger, and white pepper and cook, stirring constantly, for 3–4 minutes, until thickened. Serve immediately with Light Egg Fried Rice (see page 224) or steamed rice.

For Chinese-style spicy green beans, trim 1 lb stringless green beans and cut into 1 inch lengths. Cook in a large saucepan of lightly salted boiling water for 3–4 minutes. Drain and set aside. Place 2 seeded and chopped red chiles, 4 coarsely chopped shallots, 2 coarsely chopped garlic cloves, 2 teaspoons peeled and grated fresh ginger root, and ¼ cup light soy sauce in a blender and process to a smooth paste, adding a little water, if needed, to loosen the mixture. Spray a nonstick wok or skillet with low-calorie cooking spray and heat over medium heat. Add the chili paste and stir-fry for 2–3 minutes, until fragrant. Add the drained green beans and stir-fry for 2–3 minutes, until just tender. Serve immediately with Light Egg Fried Rice (see page 224).

tofu & asparagus stir-fry

Serves **4**

Preparation time **15 minutes**

Cooking time **15 minutes**

1 lb **asparagus tips**

4 **garlic cloves**, crushed

2 **red chiles**, seeded and
thinly sliced

good pinch of **sea salt**

1 tablespoon **peanut oil**

13 oz **firm tofu**, drained and
cut into bite-size pieces

1 cup **roasted cashew nuts**

3 tablespoons **dark soy sauce**

1 tablespoon packed **light
brown sugar**

small handful of **cilantro
leaves**, chopped

salt

Bring a large saucepan of lightly salted water to a boil,
add the asparagus, and blanch for 2–3 minutes. Drain
and set aside.

Place the garlic, 1 of the chiles, and the sea salt in a
mortar and crush with a pestle to make a paste.

Heat a nonstick wok or skillet over high heat. Add the
oil and heat until it starts to shimmer, then add the garlic
and chili paste and the remaining sliced chile and stir-fry
for 15 seconds, until lightly golden.

Add the tofu to the pan and stir-fry until golden, then
add the blanched asparagus and cashew nuts and
stir-fry for 4–5 minutes, until just cooked. Stir in the soy
sauce and sugar and stir-fry for another 30 seconds
before stirring in the cilantro. Serve immediately with
lime wedges and steamed rice.

For asparagus fried rice, follow the recipe above
to blanch 12 oz asparagus tips, then drain. Spray a
large, nonstick wok or skillet with low-calorie cooking
spray and heat over high heat. Add the blanched
asparagus and stir-fry for 1–2 minutes. Add 1 cup
jasmine rice or long-grain rice, freshly cooked and
cooled, 2 tablespoons each sweet chili sauce and light
soy sauce, and 1 tablespoon hot chili sauce. Stir-fry
for 3–4 minutes, until the rice is piping hot. Serve
immediately in warm bowls.

chinese wok-fried green beans

Serves **4**
Preparation time **15 minutes**
Cooking time **15 minutes**

low-calorie cooking spray
2 **garlic cloves**, thinly sliced
1 **red chile**, seeded and
thinly sliced
thumb-size piece of **fresh
ginger root**, peeled and
finely shredded
6 **scallions**, thinly sliced
6 canned **water chestnuts**,
rinsed, drained, and thinly
sliced
3 cups **green beans**
1 tablespoon **Chinese
rice wine**
¼ cup **light soy sauce**
¼ cup **hot water**
2 teaspoons **sesame oil**
⅓ cup **roasted peanuts**,
coarsely chopped
white pepper

Spray a large, nonstick wok or skillet with cooking spray and heat over high heat. Add the garlic and chile and stir-fry for a few seconds. Add the ginger, the scallions, and water chestnuts and stir-fry for 30 seconds.

Add the green beans to the pan and stir-fry for 5–6 minutes, until they begin to blister and turn slightly brown. Add the rice wine and soy sauce and cook for another 20–30 seconds.

Pour in the measured water and leave the vegetables to steam for 4–5 minutes, until the water has almost evaporated and the beans are cooked through but still crunchy. Stir in the sesame oil, then serve immediately, sprinkled with the roasted peanuts.

For stir-fry snow peas with sesame & garlic, spray a nonstick wok or large skillet with cooking spray and heat over high heat Add 1 lb snow peas and stir-fry for 2–3 minutes. Add 3 finely diced garlic cloves and stir-fry for 1 minute. Stir in 1 teaspoon sugar and stir-fry for 10 seconds. Pour in 1¼ cups vegetable stock and simmer for 2 minutes, or until the snow peas are just tender. Stir in 1 teaspoon sesame oil and serve.

egg foo yung

Serves **4**
Preparation time **30 minutes**
Cooking time **45–55 minutes**

low-calorie cooking spray
8 **scallions**, finely chopped
2 **garlic cloves**, crushed
1 teaspoon peeled and grated
   fresh ginger root
3 cups shredded **cabbage**
1 (8 oz) can diced **water
   chestnuts**
7 oz **shiitake mushrooms**,
   finely chopped
1 **red bell pepper**, seeded
   and finely chopped
½ cup **bean sprouts**
8 **eggs**
1 teaspoon **dark soy sauce**
¼ cup **chives**, chopped
1 **red chile**, finely chopped
salt and **black pepper**

Sauce
1¾ cups **vegetable stock**
¼ cup **tomato paste**
3 tablespoons **dark soy sauce**
2 tablespoons **hoisin sauce**
1 tablespoon **cornstarch**,
   mixed to a paste with
   2 tablespoons **cold water**

Spray a large, nonstick skillet with cooking spray and heat over high heat. Add the scallions, garlic, ginger, cabbage, water chestnuts, mushrooms, red bell pepper, and bean sprouts and stir-fry for 8–10 minutes, until the vegetables are lightly browned and softened. Transfer to a large bowl and let cool

Beat the eggs with the soy sauce, chives, and chile in a bowl, season with salt and black pepper, and then pour into the cooled vegetable mixture. Stir to mix well.

Spray an 8½ inch nonstick skillet with cooking spray and heat over medium-high heat. Add one quarter of the egg mixture, swirl to coat the bottom of the pan, and cook for 5–6 minutes, until the underside is set. Carefully flip over and cook for 3–4 minutes, until cooked. Remove and keep warm. Repeat with the remaining egg mixture.

Meanwhile, for the sauce, put the stock, tomato paste, soy sauce, and hoisin sauce into a small saucepan and bring to a boil. Add the cornstarch paste and cook over high heat, stirring constantly, for 3–4 minutes, until thickened. Transfer each pancake to a warm serving plate, spoon the sauce over them, and serve.

For cabbage, mushroom & red pepper stir-fry, spray a large, nonstick wok with low-calorie cooking spray and heat. Add 2 teaspoons each of grated garlic and fresh ginger root, 4 sliced scallions, 3 cups shredded cabbage, 7 oz sliced shiitake mushrooms, and 2 seeded and sliced red bell peppers. Stir-fry for 3–4 minutes and then add 1 (8 oz) can water chestnuts, drained and sliced, and ½ cup bean sprouts. Stir in 2 tablespoons each of dark soy sauce and sweet chili sauce and toss until mixed and heated through. Serve.

sweet chili vegetable stir-fry

Serves **4**

Preparation time **20 minutes**

Cooking time **15 minutes**

low-calorie cooking spray

4 **garlic cloves**, thinly sliced

1 teaspoon peeled and finely chopped **fresh ginger root**

8 **scallions**, diagonally sliced

3 cups thinly sliced **napa cabbage**

1 **carrot**, cut into matchsticks

1½ cups **broccoli florets**

2 cups **sugar snap peas**

½ cup **bean sprouts**

8 **baby corn**, halved lengthwise

½ cup **vegetable stock**

⅓ cup **sweet chili sauce**

¼ cup **light soy sauce**

1 teaspoon **sesame oil**

½ cup **roasted cashew nuts**

2 tablespoons seeded and diced **red chile**

Spray a large, nonstick wok or skillet with cooking spray and heat over high heat. Add the garlic, ginger, scallions, and cabbage and stir-fry for 1–2 minutes.

Add the carrot, broccoli, sugar snap peas, bean sprouts, and baby corn to the pan and continue to stir-fry for 4–5 minutes, until the vegetables are slightly softened.

Stir in the stock, bring to a boil, and cook for 3–4 minutes.

Mix together the sweet chili sauce, soy sauce, and sesame oil in a small bowl and pour the sauce over the vegetables. Cook, stirring, for 1–2 minutes.

Sprinkle with the cashew nuts and chile and serve with steamed rice or egg noodles.

For quick vegetable, noodle & sweet chili stir-fry,

spray a nonstick wok or skillet with cooking spray and heat over high heat. Add 1 (12 oz) package stir-fry vegetables and stir-fry for 3–4 minutes. Stir in 12 oz fresh egg noodles and ⅓ cup each of sweet chili sauce and water. Cook, stirring, for 2–3 minutes, until the noodles are piping hot. Serve immediately.

buddha's delight

Serves **4**

Preparation time **20 minutes**,
    plus marinating

Cooking time **15 minutes**

¼ cup **light soy sauce**

1 teaspoon **sesame oil**

1 tablespoon **rice vinegar**

2 teaspoons **honey**

13 oz **firm tofu**, drained and
    cut into 1 inch cubes

4 cups **broccoli florets**

2 **carrots**, halved lengthwise
    and thinly sliced diagonally

low-calorie cooking spray

1 **onion**, halved and thinly sliced

8 **scallions**, diagonally sliced
    into 1¼ inch lengths

1 tablespoon peeled and
    grated **fresh ginger root**

2 **garlic cloves**, crushed

3 cups **snow peas**

12 **baby corn**, thinly sliced

1 (8 oz) can **water chestnuts**,
    rinsed and drained

1 tablespoon **cornstarch**

1 cup **vegetable stock**

Mix together the soy sauce, sesame oil, rice vinegar, and honey in a glass or ceramic bowl, add the tofu, and toss to coat. Cover and let marinate in the refrigerator for 1 hour. Drain the tofu, reserving the marinade.

Meanwhile, bring a large saucepan of water to a boil, add the broccoli florets and carrots, and blanch for 2 minutes. Drain and then plunge the vegetables into a bowl of iced water. Drain again and set aside.

Spray a nonstick wok or large skillet with cooking spray and heat over medium-high heat. Add the marinated tofu and stir-fry for 5 minutes, until lightly browned. Add the onion, scallions, ginger, and garlic and stir-fry for 30 seconds. Stir the blanched broccoli and carrot into the pan along with the snow peas, baby corn, and water chestnuts and stir-fry for 1–2 minutes.

Mix together the cornstarch, stock, and reserved marinade in a small bowl until smooth and add to the pan. Bring to a boil and cook, stirring constantly, for 2–3 minutes, until slightly thickened. Serve with rice or noodles.

For tofu & vegetable stir-fry, spray a large, nonstick wok or skillet with cooking spray, add 1 tablespoon sesame oil, and heat over medium heat. Add 12 oz firm tofu, drained and cut into 1 inch cubes, and stir-fry for 1–2 minutes, until browned. Add 2 thinly sliced garlic cloves and stir-fry for 1 minute. Add 1⅓ cups of peeled and blanched fava beans, 2 cups coarsely chopped snow peas, and 1 finely chopped red chile and stir-fry for 1 minute. Spoon the vegetables onto warm plates and sprinkle with 3 tablespoons light soy sauce. Serve with steamed rice.

braised tofu with eggplant

Serves **4**
Preparation time **15 minutes**
Cooking time **15 minutes**

1 tablespoon **peanut oil**
1 large **eggplant**, cut into
   finger-thick batons
2–3 tablespoons **water**
2 **garlic cloves**, finely chopped
1 tablespoon peeled and finely
   chopped **fresh ginger root**
1 small **red chile**, seeded and
   finely chopped
1 tablespoon **chili bean paste**
1 cup boiling **vegetable stock**
7 oz **firm tofu**, drained and cut
   into bite-size squares
2 tablespooons **light
   soy sauce**
1 tablespoon **black rice
   vinegar**
2 teaspoons packed **light
   brown sugar**
6 **scallions**, thinly sliced, plus
   extra to garnish
1 tablespoon **cornstarch**,
   mixed to a paste with
   2 tablespoons **cold water**

Heat a nonstick wok or large skillet over high heat
and add half the oil. Add the eggplant and stir-fry for
5–6 minutes, until browned and softened. Add the
measured water and cook for 1–2 minutes. Transfer
the eggplant to a plate and set aside.

Add the remaining oil to the pan and heat over high
heat. Add the garlic, ginger, and chile and stir, then add
the chili bean paste and stir-fry for 30 seconds.

Pour in the hot stock, return the eggplant to the pan
along with the tofu, and bring to a simmer. Add the soy
sauce, vinegar, and sugar, then stir in the scallions and
the cornstarch paste and cook, stirring constantly, for
3–4 minutes, until the mixture has thickened. Sprinkle
with scallions and serve with steamed rice.

For spicy braised eggplants, cut 1 large eggplant
into finger-thick batons. Spray a nonstick skillet with
low-calorie cooking spray and heat over high heat. Add
the eggplant and stir-fry for 5–6 minutes, until lightly
browned. Remove and drain on paper towels. Wipe the
pan clean with paper towels, respray with cooking spray,
and heat over medium heat. Add 6 coarsely chopped
scallions and 4 finely chopped garlic cloves and stir-fry
over for 6–7 minutes, until browned. Add 1 tablespoon
finely grated fresh ginger root, 2 finely chopped red
chiles, 1 cup tomato puree or tomato sauce, and
6 kaffir lime leaves and cook, stirring, for 2–3 minutes.
Return the eggplant to the pan with a splash of water
and simmer for 2–3 minutes. Stir in 1 tablespoon each
of kecap manis, light soy sauce, honey, lime juice, and
chopped cilantro. Sprinkle with a handful of chopped
roasted peanuts and serve with rice or noodles.

bok choy with chile & ginger

Serves **4**

Preparation time **5 minutes**

Cooking time **5 minutes**

1 tablespoon **peanut oil**

½ **red chile,** sliced into rings

1 tablespoon peeled and
   chopped **fresh ginger root**

large pinch of **salt**

1 lb **bok choy,** leaves
   separated

½ cup **water**

¼ teaspoon **sesame oil**

Heat the oil in a nonstick wok or large skillet over high
heat until the oil starts to shimmer. Add the chile, ginger,
and salt and stir-fry for 15 seconds.

Add the bok choy to the pan and stir-fry for 1 minute,
then add the measured water and continue to cook,
stirring, until the bok choy is tender and the water
has evaporated.

Toss in the sesame oil and serve immediately.

**For bok choy & shiiitake mushrooms with chile,
ginger & oyster sauce**, follow the recipe above, adding
8 oz trimmed and sliced shiitake mushrooms with the
bok choy and stirring 2 tablespoons oyster sauce into
the pan with the water.

vegetable stir-fry with bok choy

Serves **4**
Preparation time **10 minutes**
Cooking time **10 minutes**

8 baby **bok choy**
1 tablespoon **peanut oil**
2 **garlic cloves**, thinly sliced
1 inch piece of **fresh ginger
  root**, peeled and finely
  chopped
3 cups diagonally sliced
  sugar snap peas
8 oz **asparagus tips**, halved
  lengthwise
12 **baby corn**, halved
  lengthwise
1 cup **edamame (soybeans)**
  or 2 cups **bean sprouts**
⅔ cup **sweet teriyaki sauce**

Cut the bok choy in half, or into thick slices if large. Put into a bamboo steamer, cover ,and steam over a wok or large saucepan of boiling water (see page 14) for 2–3 minutes, until tender. Drain and keep warm.

Heat a large, nonstick wok or skillet over high heat, add the oil, garlic, and ginger, and stir-fry for 30 seconds. Add the sugar snap peas, asparagus tips, baby corn, and edamame or bean sprouts and stir-fry for 2–3 minutes, until softened.

Pour over the sweet teriyaki sauce and toss together until heated through. Serve immediately with the steamed bok choy and steamed rice, if desired.

For sweet chili vegetable stir-fry, heat a large, nonstick wok or skillet over high heat, add 1 tablespoon peanut oil, 1 thinly sliced onion, 2 thinly sliced garlic cloves, and a 1 inch)piece of fresh ginger root, peeled and finely chopped, and stir-fry for 30 seconds. Add 1 carrot, cut into thin matchsticks, and 3 cups sliced mushrooms and stir-fry for 2 minutes. Stir in 2 cups bean sprouts and 5 cups shredded spinach and stir-fry for about 1 minute, until wilted. Add 1 cup sweet chili sauce and toss together until heated through. Serve immediately with the steamed bok choy as in the recipe above or noodles.

rice &
noodles

eggplant & sesame noodle salad

Serves **4**

Preparation time **30 minutes**, plus cooling

Cooking time **30 minutes**

2 **eggplants**

1 teaspoon **chili oil**

¼ cup **sesame oil**

⅓ cup **light soy sauce**

¼ cup **sweet chili sauce**

2 tablespoons **Chinese rice wine**

3 tablespoons **honey**

3 tablespoons **sesame seeds**, toasted

6 oz **dried fine egg noodles**

1 teaspoon peeled and finely chopped **fresh ginger root**

1 **garlic clove**, crushed

(1 cup **baby spinach leaves**

1 **red bell pepper**, seeded and finely chopped

8 **scallions**, thinly sliced

½ cup **bean sprouts**

large handful of coarsely chopped **cilantro leaves**

Prick each eggplant all over with a fork, put onto a baking sheet, and bake in a preheated oven, at 400°F, for 30 minutes, or until softened. Let cool.

Meanwhile, mix together the oils, soy sauce, sweet chili sauce, rice wine, and honey in a bowl. Stir in the sesame seeds and divide the dressing between 2 wide bowls.

Cook the noodles in a saucepan of boiling water for about 3 minutes, or according to the package directions, until just tender. Drain, add to one of the bowls of dressing, and toss to coat evenly.

Mix the ginger and garlic into the remaining bowl of dressing.

Cut the eggplants in half lengthwise, then peel away and discard the skin. Using a spoon, scoop the flesh into the bowl of garlicky dressing. Stir in the spinach, red bell pepper, scallions, and bean sprouts, then add the dressed noodles and toss to mix well. Sprinkle with the cilantro and serve.

For zucchini & sesame noodle stir-fry, spray a large, nonstick wok or skillet with low-calorie cooking spray and heat over high heat. Add 2 teaspoons each of grated fresh ginger root and garlic, 1 teaspoon sesame oil, 2 coarsely grated zucchini, and 1 cored, seeded and finely chopped red bell pepper and stir-fry for 2–3 minutes, then stir in 1 lb fresh egg noodles. Add ¼ cup light soy sauce and 3 tablespoons sweet chili sauce and cook, tossing, for 2–3 minutes, or according to the package directions, until the noodles are just tender. Serve in warm bowls.

beef & vegetable fried rice

Serves **4**
Preparation time **10 minutes**
Cooking time **10 minutes**

2 tablespoons **peanut oil**
2 **garlic cloves**, crushed
2 **Thai chiles**, finely chopped
2 **shallots**, cut into thin
   wedges
8 oz **lean tenderloin steak**,
   cut into thin strips
1 **green bell pepper**, seeded
   and cut into strips
8 **baby corn**, halved
   lengthwise
4 oz **straw mushrooms**,
   trimmed
2 tablespoons **Thai fish sauce**
½ teaspoon **demerara sugar**
   or **other raw sugar**
1 tablespoon **light soy sauce**
½ cup **jasmine rice** or
   long-grain rice, freshly
   cooked and cooled
4 **scallions**, cut into thin slices
handful of **cilantro leaves**, torn

Heat the oil in a nonstick wok or large skillet over high heat until the oil starts to shimmer. Add the garlic, chiles, shallots, and steak and stir-fry for 2–3 minutes, until the beef begins to brown.

Add the green bell pepper, baby corn, and mushrooms and stir-fry for 2 minutes.

Stir the Thai fish sauce, sugar, and soy sauce into the pan and cook for a few more seconds, then add the rice and scallions and toss together for 1–2 minutes, until the rice is piping hot. Stir in the cilantro and serve.

For mixed vegetable fried rice, follow the recipe above, omitting the beef and stir-frying the garlic, chile, and shallots for a few seconds, then stir in the remaining vegetables as above, adding 1½ cups sliced broccoli florets and ¾ cup bean sprouts. Continue with the recipe as above.

noodles with preserved cabbage

Serves **4**
Preparation time **15 minutes**
Cooking time **10 minutes**

low-calorie cooking spray
3½ oz canned **Sichuan preserved cabbage**, rinsed, drained, and finely chopped
4 **garlic cloves**, finely chopped
2 teaspoons peeled and finely chopped **fresh ginger root**
2 tablespoons **Chinese rice wine**
2 tablespoons **chili bean sauce**
1 tablespoon **Chinese sesame paste**
1 tablespoon **dark soy sauce**
1 tablespoon **honey**
2 cups **chicken stock** or **vegetable stock**
8 oz **dried medium egg noodles**

Spray a large, nonstick wok or skillet with cooking spray and heat over high heat. Add the preserved cabbage, garlic, and ginger and stir-fry for 1–2 minutes.

Stir all the remaining ingredients except the noodles into the pan, reduce the heat to medium, and simmer for 3–4 minutes.

Meanwhile, cook the noodles in a large saucepan of boiling water for about 4 minutes, or according to the package directions, until just tender.

Drain the noodles and divide among 4 warm bowls. Ladle the cabbage mixture over the noodles and serve immediately.

For stir-fried rice with preserved cabbage, baby corn & bean sprouts, spray a large, nonstick wok or skillet with low-calorie cooking spray and heat over medium-high heat. Add 2 teaspoons each grated fresh ginger root and garlic and stir-fry for 30 seconds. Add 3½ oz canned Sichuan preserved cabbage, rinsed, drained, and finely chopped, 6 sliced baby corn, 1½ cups snow peas, and 1 cup bean sprouts and stir–fry for 3–4 minutes. Stir in 1 cup jasmine rice or long-grain rice, freshly cooked and cooled, ¼ cup light soy sauce, and 1 teaspoon chili bean paste and toss together for 1–2 minutes, until the rice is piping hot. Serve immediately.

ants climbing a tree

Serves **4**

Preparation time **15 minutes**, plus standing

Cooking time **15 minutes**

8 oz **dried fine cellophane noodles**

1 tablespoon **peanut oil**

1 tablespoon peeled and finely grated **fresh ginger root**

3 **garlic cloves**, crushed

6 **shiitake mushrooms**, trimmed and thinly sliced

2 **red chiles**, seeded and finely chopped

8 **scallions**, finely chopped

12 oz **ground pork**

2 tablespoons **dark soy sauce**

2 tablespoons **hoisin sauce**

1 cup boiling **chicken stock** or **vegetable stock**

1 tablespoon **cornstarch**, mixed to a paste with 2 tablespoons **cold water**

7 oz **firm tofu**, drained and cut into bite-size cubes

Put the noodles into a large heatproof bowl, pour over enough boiling hot water to cover, and let stand for 10 minutes, or prepare according to the package directions, until just tender. Drain and set aside.

Meanwhile, heat the oil in a large, nonstick wok or skillet over high heat. Add the ginger, garlic, mushrooms, chiles, and scallions and stir-fry for 1–2 minutes. Add the ground pork and stir-fry, breaking it up with a wooden spoon, for 4–5 minutes, until browned.

Stir the soy sauce, hoisin sauce, and stock into the pan and cook for 2 minutes. Add the cornstarch paste and cook, stirring constantly, for 2–3 minutes, until thickened.

Add the drained noodles and tofu and toss together for 2–3 minutes, until heated through. Serve immediately.

For chicken & hoisin sauce fried rice, spray a large, nonstick wok or skillet with low-calorie cooking spray and heat over high heat. Add 2 teaspoons each of grated fresh ginger root and garlic, 2 finely chopped red chiles, and 12 oz ground chicken and stir-fry, breaking up the chicken with a wooden spoon, for 2–3 minutes, until the chicken is lightly browned. Stir in 6 finely chopped scallions, 1 cup jasmine rice or long-grain rice, freshly cooked and cooled, and 2 tablespoons hoisin sauce and cook, stirring, for 6–7 minutes, until the rice is piping hot. Serve in warm bowls, garnished with thinly sliced scallions.

broccoli & mushroom fried rice

Serves **4**

Preparation time **20 minutes**

Cooking time **15 minutes**

4 cups thin **baby broccoli** slices (cut lengthwise)

2 **carrots**, cut into thin matchsticks

4 extra-large **eggs**

2 tablespoons **cold water**

low-calorie cooking spray

1 tablespoon peeled and grated **fresh ginger root**

3 **garlic cloves**, crushed

1 cup **jasmine rice** or **long-grain rice**, freshly cooked and cooled

7 oz **oyster mushrooms**, trimmed

½ cup boiling **vegetable stock**

2 tablespoons **light soy sauce**

1 teaspoon **sesame oil**

white pepper

Put the broccoli and carrots into a bamboo steamer, cover, and steam over a wok or large saucepan of boiling water (see page 14) for about 2 minutes, until tender but still crisp. Drain and set aside.

Beat the eggs with the measured water in a bowl. Spray a large, nonstick skillet or wok with cooking spray and heat over medium-high heat. Pour in the egg mixture and cook, stirring, for about 30 seconds, until softly scrambled. Remove from pan and set aside.

Wipe the pan clean with paper towels, lightly respray with cooking spray, and heat over medium heat. Add the ginger and garlic and stir-fry for 30 seconds, then add the rice and mushrooms and stir-fry over high heat for 3–4 minutes. Add the steamed broccoli and carrot and the stock and cook, stirring, for 3–4 minutes.

Return the scrambled egg to the pan with the soy sauce and sesame oil. Season with white pepper and stir-fry for 1 minute, until the egg is heated through, then serve.

For broccoli, mushroom & carrot stir-fry, mix 1 tablespoon cornstarch to a paste with 3 tablespoons cold water. Thinly slice the florets from ½ head of broccoli lengthwise. Cut 2 carrots into thin matchsticks and thinly slice 7 oz shiitake mushrooms. Spray a large, nonstick wok or skillet with low-calorie cooking spray and heat over high heat. Add the vegetables and stir-fry for 3–4 minutes. Add ⅓ cup stir-fry sauce and ½ cup water and cook, stirring, for 2–3 minutes. Stir in the cornstarch paste and cook, stirring constantly, for 2–3 minutes, until the mixture has thickened. Serve with rice or noodles.

chicken chow mein

Serves **4**

Preparation time **20 minutes**,
plus marinating

Cooking time **20 minutes**

¼ cup **light soy sauce**

1 tablespoon **hot chili sauce**

2 teaspoons **Chinese
rice wine**

4 **garlic cloves**, crushed

2 teaspoons peeled and finely
grated **fresh ginger root**

1 teaspoon **Chinese
five-spice powder**

3 **boneless chicken breasts**,
about 6 oz each, skinned
and thinly sliced

8 oz **dried fine egg noodles**

low-calorie cooking spray

3 cups **sugar snap peas**

1 (8 oz) canned **water
chestnuts**, drained and sliced

1 cup drained, canned
sliced bamboo shoots

1 **red bell pepper**, seeded
and thinly sliced

8 **scallions**, diagonally sliced
into 2 inch lengths

¼ cup **sweet chili sauce**

¼ cup **dark soy sauce**

Mix together the light soy sauce, hot chili sauce, rice
wine, garlic, ginger, and five-spice powder in a bowl.
Add the chicken and toss to coat evenly. Cover and
let marinate at room temperature for 10 minutes.

Meanwhile, cook the noodles in a saucepan of boiling
water for about 3 minutes, or according to the package
directions, until just tender. Drain and set aside.

Spray a large, nonstick wok or skillet with cooking
spray and heat over high heat. Add the chicken mixture
and stir-fry for 4–5 minutes, until lightly browned. Add
all the vegetables and stir-fry for 4–5 minutes, until
just tender.

Add the drained noodles to the pan with the sweet chilli
sauce and dark soy sauce and toss together for 3 minutes
or until the noodles are piping hot. Serve in warm bowls.

For chicken & vegetable fried rice, spray a large,
nonstick wok or skillet with low-calorie cooking spray
and heat over high heat. Add 2 teaspoons each of
grated fresh ginger root and garlic and 12 oz ground
chicken and stir-fry, breaking up the chicken with a
wooden spoon, for 2–3 minutes, until the chicken
is lightly browned. Add 3 cups snow peas, 1 (8 oz)
canned water chestnuts, rinsed, drained, and sliced,
1 cored, seeded, and thinly sliced red bell pepper, and
6 sliced scallions and stir-fry for 2–3 minutes. Add
1 cup jasmine rice or long-grain rice, freshly cooked and
cooled, 2 tablespoons light soy sauce, and 2 teaspoons
Chinese rice wine and toss together for 2–3 minutes,
until the rice is piping hot. Serve ladled into warm bowls.

singapore noodles

Serves **4**

Preparation time **20 minutes**

Cooking time **15 minutes**

low-calorie cooking spray

1 lb **raw jumbo shrimp**, peeled and deveined

4 oz lean **rindless bacon**, cut into small pieces

3 **garlic cloves**, crushed

1 teaspoon finely grated **fresh ginger root**

1 **onion**, thinly sliced

1 **carrot**, cut into matchsticks

3 cups thinly sliced **sugar snap peas**

½ cup **bean sprouts**

1–2 tablespoons **curry powder** (medium or hot)

6 **scallions**, thinly sliced diagonally

8 oz **dried fine rice noodles**, cooked according to the package directions and drained well

about 2 tablespoons **water**

⅓ cup **dark soy sauce**

3 tablespoons **sweet chili sauce**

2 **red chiles**, seeded and thinly sliced, to garnish

salt and **black pepper**

Spray a large, nonstick wok or skillet with cooking spray and heat over high heat. Add the shrimp and bacon and stir-fry for 4–5 minutes, until the shrimp turn pink and the bacon is golden. Remove and keep warm.

Wipe out the pan with paper towels. Respray with cooking spray and heat over high heat. Add the garlic and ginger and stir-fry for 30 seconds. Add the onion, carrot, sugar snap peas, and bean sprouts and stir-fry for 2–3 minutes, until soft, then add the curry powder and scallions and cook, stirring, for 1 minute.

Add the prepared noodles with the measured water and toss everything together. Stir in the soy sauce and sweet chili sauce, season with salt and black pepper, and stir-fry for another minute. Return the shrimp and bacon to the pan with their juices and toss through the mixture.

Divide the noodle mixture among 4 warm, shallow bowls, sprinkle with the chiles, and serve with lime wedges.

For noodle & vegetable soup, divide 8 oz cooked, dried fine egg noodles among 4 warm soup bowls. Spray a nonstick wok with low-calorie cooking spray and heat until smoking. Add 1 tablespoon grated fresh ginger root and 1 thinly sliced red chile and stir-fry for a few seconds. Add 2 tablespoons Chinese rice wine and 4 cups vegetable stock and bring to a simmer. Add 8 oz thinly sliced shiitake mushrooms and 1 julienned carrot. Season with 2 tablespoons light soy sauce and 1 teaspoon each of dark soy sauce and rice vinegar. Mix 1 tablespoon cornstarch with 2 tablespoons cold water, stir into the soup, and cook for 2–3 minutes, until slightly thickened. Stir in ½ cup bean sprouts and 6 sliced scallions and heat through. Ladle over the noodles and serve.

pork & shrimp fried rice

Serves **4**

Preparation time **5 minutes**

Cooking time **5 minutes**

4 **eggs**

1 ½ teaspoons **sesame oil**

2 teaspoons **light soy sauce**

pinch of **salt**

1 tablespoon **peanut oil**

4 oz **raw, peeled shrimp**

1 cup shredded, **cooked ham**

1 tablespoon peeled and chopped **fresh ginger root**

2 **garlic cloves**, crushed

5 **scallions**, thinly sliced

½ cup **jasmine rice** or **long-grain rice**, freshly cooked and cooled

Beat the eggs with 1 teaspoon of the sesame oil, the soy sauce, and salt in a bowl until combined.

Heat ½ tablespoon of the peanut oil in a wok or large skillet over high heat until the oil starts to shimmer. Pour in the egg mixture and cook, stirring constantly, for about 30 seconds, until softly scrambled. Remove from the pan and set aside.

Return the pan to the heat and add the remaining peanut oil, then add the shrimp, ham, ginger, and garlic and stir-fry for 1 minute, until the shrimp have turned pink. Add the scallions, rice, scrambled egg, and remaining sesame oil and toss together for 1–2 minutes, until the rice is piping hot.

For chicken fried rice, follow the recipe above to cook the eggs, omitting the shrimp and ham. Remove from the pan, then heat 1 tablespoon peanut oil in the pan, add the ginger and garlic as above along with 2 cups finely chopped, skinless chicken breast, and stir-fry for 2–3 minutes, until lightly browned and cooked. Add 2 tablespoons oyster sauce and cook, stirring, for 1 minute, then add the scallions and rice and continue with the recipe as above.

pork meatball noodle stir-fry

Serves **4**
Preparation time **20 minutes**
Cooking time **20–25 minutes**

1 lb ground **pork**
2 teaspoons peeled and finely
  grated **fresh ginger root**
1 tablespoon **grated garlic**
4 **scallions**, thinly sliced
1 **red chile,** finely chopped
1 cup finely chopped **cilantro**
½ cup finely chopped **mint**
1 **egg**, beaten
1 teaspoon **salt**
1 tablespoon **kecap manis**
  (Indonesian sweet soy
  sauce)
⅓ cup **sesame seeds**
2 tablespoons **peanut oil**
3 cups 4–5 inch **choy sum**
  pieces (stems and leaves
  separated)
1 lb **fresh egg noodles**
¼ cup **light soy sauce**
⅓ cup **sweet chili sauce**

To garnish
scallion slivers
diced red chile
cilantro leaves

Put the ground pork, ginger, garlic, scallions, chile, chopped herbs, egg, salt, and kecap manis in a bowl and mix well with your fingers.

Divide the mixture into 20 portions and roll each into a ball.

Spread the sesame seeds evenly over a large plate. Roll the meatballs in the seeds to coat.

Heat 1 tablespoon of the oil in a large, nonstick wok or skillet over medium heat, add the meatballs, and cook, turning frequently, for 12–15 minutes, until browned and cooked through. Transfer to a plate with a slotted spoon and keep warm.

Wipe the pan clean with paper towels, add the remaining oil, and heat over medium-high heat. Add the choy sum stem and stir-fry for about 1–2 minutes, until just wilted. Stir in the noodles and stir-fry for 3 minutes, or until piping hot.

Mix together the soy sauce and sweet chili sauce and add to the pan with the choy sum leaves and meatballs. Toss together until heated through, then serve immediately in warm bowls, garnished with scallion, diced red chile, and cilantro leaves.

For shrimp & chicken meatball noodle stir-fry,
follow the recipe above, replacing the ground pork with 8 oz ground chicken and 8 oz raw, peeled jumbo shrimp, finely chopped.

special fried rice

Serves **4**
Preparation time **30 minutes**
Cooking time **15 minutes**

low-calorie cooking spray
3 **eggs**, lightly beaten
1 tablespoon peeled and
   finely diced **fresh ginger root**
4 **garlic cloves**, finely diced
1 **onion**, halved and thinly
   sliced
4 oz **Chinese sausage** (lap
   chong), coarsely chopped
4 oz small **cooked,
   peeled shrimp**
1 teaspoon **sugar**
2 tablespoons **Chinese
   rice wine**
1 cup **jasmine rice** or **long-
   grain rice**, freshly cooked
   and cooled
2 tablespoons **oyster sauce**
10 **scallions**, thinly sliced
3 tablespoons **light soy sauce**
1 teaspoon **sesame oil**

Spray a large, nonstick wok or skillet with cooking spray and heat over high heat. Pour in the beaten eggs and swirl to coat the bottom of the pan evenly. Cook for about 1 minute, until almost cooked through and just set. Carefully remove the omelet from the pan and drain on paper towels.

Roll the omelet into a log shape, thinly slice into thin strips and set aside.

Wipe the pan clean with paper towels, respray with cooking spray, and heat over medium heat. Add the ginger and garlic and stir-fry for 30 seconds. Add the onion and Chinese sausage and stir-fry for 2–3 minutes, until lightly browned and tender. Add the shrimp and stir-fry for 30 seconds. Stir in the sugar and rice wine and cook, stirring, for 1 minute.

Add the rice, reserved omelet strips, oyster sauce, scallions, soy sauce, and sesame oil to the pan and toss together for 3–4 minutes, until the rice is piping hot. Divide the rice mixture among 4 warm bowls and serve immediately.

For shrimp fried noodles, spray a large, nonstick wok or skillet with low-calorie cooking spray and heat over high heat. Add 2 teaspoons each of grated fresh ginger root and garlic, 6 sliced scallions, 1 coarsely grated zucchini, and 1 seeded and finely chopped red bell pepper and stir-fry for 2–3 minutes. Add 1 lb fresh egg noodles, 8 oz cooked, peeled shrimp, ¼ cup light soy sauce, 1 tablespoon sweet chili sauce, and 1 teaspoon sesame oil and toss together for 2–3 minutes, until the noodles and shrimp are piping hot. Serve immediately.

lamb & bok choy noodle stir-fry

Serves **4**

Preparation time **15 minutes**

Cooking time about **10 minutes**

8 oz **dried fine egg noodles**

1 teaspoon **cornstarch**

1 tablespoon **light soy sauce**

1 tablespoon **oyster sauce**

2 tablespoons **Chinese rice wine**

2 teaspoons **rice vinegar**

low-calorie cooking spray

10 oz boneless lean **lamb cutlets**, cut into thin strips

2 teaspoons peeled and finely chopped **fresh ginger root**

2 heads of **bok choy**, cut into wide strips

8 **scallions**, thinly sliced

1 cup **bean sprouts**

1 teaspoon **sesame oil**

1 teaspoon **chili oil**

Cook the noodles in a large saucepan of boiling water for about 3 minutes, or according to the package directions, until just tender. Drain and set aside.

Mix together the cornstarch, soy sauce, oyster sauce, rice wine, and vinegar in a small bowl.

Spray a large, nonstick wok or skillet with cooking spray and heat over high heat. Add the lamb and stir-fry for 2–3 minutes, until just cooked. Remove with a slotted spoon and set aside. Add the ginger, bok choy, scallions, and bean sprouts to the pan and stir-fry for 2–3 minutes, until slightly softened.

Return the lamb to the pan along with the drained noodles, sauce mixture, the sesame oil, and chili oil. Toss together for 1–2 minutes, until heated through and serve immediately.

For broiled lamb with oyster sauce and noodles,

put 8 boneless, lean lamb cutlets into a glass or ceramic dish in a single layer. Mix together ⅓ cup oyster sauce, 2 tablespoons sweet chili sauce, and 2 teaspoons peeled and grated fresh ginger root. Spread over the cutlets to coat evenly. Place the cutlets on a broiler rack and cook under a preheated medium-high broiler for 4–5 minutes on each side, or until cooked to your preference. Serve with cooked egg noodles and Chinese steamed greens.

light egg fried rice

Serves **4**
Preparation time **5 minutes**
Cooking time **5 minutes**

4 eggs
2 teaspoons peeled and
    chopped **fresh ginger root**
1 ½ tablespoons **light soy
    sauce**
2 tablespoons **peanut oil**
½ cup **jasmine rice** or **long-
    grain rice**, freshly cooked
    and cooled
2 **scallions**, thinly sliced
¼ teaspoon **sesame oil**

Beat the eggs with the ginger and half the soy sauce in a bowl until combined.

Heat the oil in a nonstick wok or large skillet over high heat until the oil starts to shimmer. Pour in the egg mixture and cook, stirring constantly, for 30 seconds or until softly scrambled.

Add the cooked rice, scallions, sesame oil, and remaining soy sauce to the pan and toss together for 1–2 minutes, until the rice is piping hot. Serve immediately.

For fried rice with Chinese greens & chile, follow the recipe above, adding 1 seeded and sliced red chile and 1 ½ cup shredded Chinese greens once the rice is piping hot and tossing together for another 30 seconds.

choy sum noodles with beef

Serves **4**
Preparation time **15 minutes**
Cooking time **10 minutes**

8 oz **dried medium egg
noodles**
10 oz lean **sirloin steak**,
trimmed of all visible fat
2 tablespoons **light soy sauce**
2 tablespoons **oyster sauce**
2 tablespoons **Chinese
rice wine**
2 teaspoons **rice vinegar**
low-calorie cooking spray
1 tablespoon peeled and finely
grated **fresh ginger root**
3 cups wide **choy sum** strips
8 **scallions**, diagonally sliced
into ½ inch lengths
1 cup **bean sprouts**
1 teaspoon **sesame oil**
salt and **black pepper**

Cook the noodles in a large saucepan of boiling water
for about 4 minutes, or according to the package
directions, until just tender. Drain and set aside.

Cut the steak into thin slices about ½ inch wide.
Spread out the beef on a plate and season with salt
and black pepper.

Mix together the soy sauce, oyster sauce, rice wine, and
vinegar in a small bowl and set aside.

Spray a large, nonstick wok or skillet with cooking
spray and heat over high heat. Add the steak and
stir-fry for 1–2 minutes, until just cooked. Remove with
a slotted spoon and set aside. Add the ginger, choy sum,
scallions, and bean sprouts and stir-fry for 1–2 minutes.

Return the steak to the pan along with the drained
noodles, sauce mixture, and the sesame oil. Toss
together for 1–2 minutes, until heated through. Serve
in warm bowls.

For garlic & ginger stir-fried choy sum, spray a large,
nonstick wok or skillet with low-calorie cooking spray
and heat over high heat. Add 1 tablespoon each of
finely chopped fresh ginger root and garlic and 1 finely
chopped red chile and stir-fry for 30 seconds. Add
7 cups coarsely chopped choy sum, 1½ (8 oz) cans
water chestnuts, rinsed, drained, and sliced, ¼ cup
light soy sauce, and 1 teaspoon sesame oil. Stir-fry
for 1–2 minutes, until the choy sum has just wilted.
Serve immediately.

tofu & shiitake egg noodles

Serves **4**
Preparation time **20 minutes**
Cooking time **15 minutes**

low-calorie cooking spray
12 oz **firm tofu**, drained and
   cut into ¾ inch cubes
¼ cup **oyster sauce**
2 tablespoons **dark soy sauce**
1 tablespoon **cornstarch**,
   mixed to a paste with
   2 tablespoons **cold water**
2 tablespoons **Chinese
   rice wine**
1 cup **vegetable stock**
2 teaspoons grated **fresh
   ginger root**
6 **scallions**, diagonally sliced
   into ¾ inch lengths, plus
   extra to garnish
1 **red chile,** finely chopped
½ **red bell pepper**, seeded
   and cut into thick strips
½ **yellow bell pepper**, seeded
   and cut into thick strips
8 oz **shiitake mushrooms**,
   trimmed and thickly sliced
12 oz **fresh egg noodles**,
   cooked according to the
   package directions

Spray a large, nonstick wok or skillet with cooking spray and heat over high heat. Add the tofu and stir-fry for 3–4 minutes, until golden. Remove and drain on paper towels.

Mix together the oyster sauce, soy sauce, cornstarch paste, rice wine, and stock in a small bowl until smooth.

Wipe the pan clean with paper towels, respray with cooking spray, and heat over high heat. Add the ginger, scallions, chile, bell peppers, and mushrooms and stir-fry for 3–4 minutes. Add the sauce mixture and bring to a boil, stirring constantly. Reduce the heat, return the tofu to the pan, and simmer gently, stirring occaisionally, for 2–3 minutes.

Add the cooked noodles and toss together for 1–2 minutes, until piping hot. Serve in warm bowls, garnished with sliced scallion.

For shiitake & scallion stir-fry, spray a large, nonstick wok or skillet with low-calorie cooking spray and heat over high heat. Add 12 oz trimmed and thickly sliced shiitake mushrooms and stir-fry for 4–5 minutes, until softened. Stir in 2 teaspoons each of finely grated fresh ginger root and garlic, 8 thickly sliced scallions, ¼ cup hoisin sauce, and ⅓ cup water and bring to a boil. Mix 1 tablespoon cornstarch to a paste with 3 tablespoons cold water, add to the pan, and cook, stirring constantly, for 2–3 minutes, until the mixture has thickened. Remove from the heat and serve with steamed rice.

noodles with shrimp & bok choy

Serves **4**

Preparation time **5 minutes**

Cooking time **15 minutes**

8 oz **dried medium egg noodles**

3 tablespoons **vegetable oil**

2 tablespoons **sesame seeds**

1 inch piece of **fresh ginger root**, peeled and finely chopped

1 **garlic clove**, crushed

20 **raw, peeled jumbo shrimp**

3 tablespoons **light soy sauce**

2 tablespoons **sweet chili sauce**

2 heads of **bok choy**, leaves separated

4 **scallions**, thinly sliced

2 tablespoons **sesame oil**

Cook the noodles in a large saucepan of boiling water for about 4 minutes, or according to the package directions, until just tender. Drain and set aside.

Add 2 tablespoons of the vegetable oil to a large, nonstick skillet and heat until almost smoking. Add the noodles so that they cover the bottom of the pan. Cook for 3–4 minutes, until golden brown and crispy on the underside. Turn over and cook on the other side until browned. Sprinkle with the sesame seeds.

Heat the remaining vegetable oil in a wok or separate large skillet, add the ginger and garlic, and stir-fry for 1 minute, then add the shrimp and stir-fry for 2 minutes, until beginning to turn pink. Add the soy sauce and sweet chili sauce, bring to a boil, then reduce the heat and simmer for 1–2 minutes, until the shrimp have turned pink. Add the bok choy and cook, stirring, until the leaves wilt.

Divide the noodles among 4 warm bowls and top with the shrimp and bok choy. Sprinkle with the scallions, drizzle with the sesame oil, and serve immediately.

For shrimp & lemon grass stir-fry, heat 1 tablespoon vegetable oil in a large wok or skillet over high heat. Add 2 finely chopped shallots, 2 finely chopped lemon grass stalks, 1 seeded and finely chopped red chile, 1 crushed garlic clove, and a ¾ inch piece of fresh ginger root, peeled and finely chopped, and stir-fry for 2 minutes. Add 20 raw, peeled jumbo shrimp and stir-fry until they turn pink. Add ⅓ cup light soy sauce, 2 tablespoons sesame oil, and the juice of 1 lime and heat through, stirring. Sprinkle with 2 tablespoons coarsely chopped cilantro and serve.

tofu & vegetable fried rice

Serves **4**

Preparation time **15 minutes**

Cooking time **15 minutes**

low-calorie cooking spray

1 **red onion**, cut into thin
  wedges

2 **garlic cloves**, finely chopped

1 **red chile,** seeded and finely
  chopped

1 **carrot**, cut into thin
  matchsticks

12 **baby corn**, diagonally
  sliced

1 head of **bok choy**, stems
  and leaves separated

12 **cherry tomatoes**, halved

1 cup **jasmine rice** or **long-
  grain rice**, freshly cooked
  and cooled

2 tablespoons **sweet
  chili sauce**

2 tablespoons **light soy sauce**

7 oz **firm tofu**, drained and cut
  into bite-size cubes

large handful of **cilantro** and
  mint leaves, finely chopped

Spray a large, nonstick wok or skillet with cooking spray and heat over high heat. Add the onion and stir-fry for 1–2 minutes, until slightly softened. Add the garlic and chile and stir-fry for about 1 minute, until aromatic.

Add the carrot, baby corn, bok choy stems, and tomatoes to the pan and stir-fry for about 3 minutes, until softened. Transfer to a bowl.

Wipe the pan clean with paper towels, respray with cooking spray, and heat over high heat. Add the cooked rice and stir-fry for 3–4 minutes, until piping hot. Add the bok choy leaves, sweet chili sauce, and soy sauce with the reserved vegetables and toss together briefly until heated through. Remove from the heat and stir in the tofu and herbs. Ladle into warm bowls and serve.

For marinated tofu with mushrooms & broccoli,

mix together 3 tablespoons each Chinese rice wine and light soy sauce, 2 tablespoons sweet chili sauce, 2 teaspoons grated fresh ginger root, 1 teaspoon grated garlic, and the juice of 1 lime in a large glass or ceramic bowl. Add 12 oz firm tofu, drained and cut into 1 inch cubes, and toss to coat evenly. Cover and let marinate for 1 hour, turning occasionally. Spray a large, nonstick wok or large skillet with low-calorie cooking spray and heat over high heat. Add 8 oz shiitake mushrooms, trimmed and thinly sliced, and stir-fry for 3–4 minutes. Add 4 cups thinly sliced broccoli florets and continue to stir-fry for 2–3 minutes. Add ½ cup hot water with the tofu and the marinade. Stir gently to mix, cover and simmer for 4–5 minutes, until the vegetables are just tender. Serve with rice.

index

acknowledgments

Executive editor: Eleanor Maxfield
Senior editor: Sybella Stephens
Text editor: Jo Richardson
Art direction and design: Penny Stock
Photographer: William Shaw
Home economist: Sunil Vijayakar
Prop stylist: Liz Hippisley
Production controller: Sarah Kramer

Photography copyright © Octopus Publishing Group
Limited/William Shaw 2014 , except the following
copyright © Octopus Publishing Group/Stephen
Conroy 45, 59, 133, 157, 173; Will Heap 73, 83, 91,
107, 197, 205, 217, 225; David Munns 55, 57, 231;
Lis Parsons 41, 77, 121; Bill Reavell 85, 115, 149;
Ian Wallace 29, 31, 139.